Patrick Bishop is twenty-nine years old. He was educated at Wimbledon College and Corpus Christi College, Oxford, and joined the *Observer* in 1979. He travelled to the Falklands with 3 Commando Brigade on board SS *Canberra*, and moved on to the islands with 42 Commando on D Day, spending much of the campaign with the unit.

John Witherow joined *The Times* in 1980 from Reuters, where he had been a correspondent in Madrid. He is thirty years old and was educated at Bedford School and York University. He sailed to the Falklands on HMS *Invincible* and joined up with the Scots and Welsh Guards at Bluff Cove from San Carlos Water.

The Winter War

The Falklands

Patrick Bishop and John Witherow

QUARTET BOOKS
LONDON MELBOURNE NEW YORK

First published by Quartet Books Limited 1982
A member of the Namara Group
27/29 Goodge Street, London W1P 1FD
Reprinted 1982 (twice)

British Library Cataloguing in Publication Data

Bishop, Patrick
  The winter war : the Falklands
  1. Falkland Islands conflict, 1982
  I. Title   II. Witherow, John
  997'.11   F3031

  ISBN 0-7043-3424-0

Typeset by MC Typeset, Rochester, Kent
Printed by Mackays of Chatham

Contents

Illustrations

Cover photograph: a memorial to those lost on *Sir Galahad*, erected by the Welsh Guards at Fitzroy, overlooking Bluff Cove (*Photograph: C.G.H. Carty*)

Troops arriving by helicopter on *Queen Elizabeth II*
Bound for Blue Beach II at San Carlos Bay
A Gurkha awaits attack
A captured 30mm anti-aircraft gun used at Goose Green
Burial of some Argentine victims at Goose Green
Sir Galahad ablaze after Sky Hawk bomb attack (*Photograph: C.G.H. Carty*)
Troops advancing against the background of Mount Harriet
Guardsmen being shelled
Casevacced out in Gazelle
Marines advancing (*Photograph: Charles Laurence*)
Victorious Scots Guards on top of Tumbledown
Paras in Port Stanley
Defeated army
Conscripts about to board *Canberra*

Photographs taken by Paul R.G. Haley, *Soldier Magazine* unless otherwise credited.

Maps reproduced by courtesy of *The Times*.

Acknowledgements

We would like to thank the following for the help they have given us with this book: Lt.-Col Hew Pike, commanding officer of the Third Battalion, the Parachute Regiment; Major Chris Keeble, of the Second Battalion, the Parachute Regiment; officers of the Special Air Service; Lt.-Col Mike Scott, commanding officer of the Second Battalion, the Scots Guards; Major Jo Griffiths-Eyton, of the First Battalion, the Welsh Guards; Commander Nigel Ward, commanding officer, 801 Harrier Squadron; and to the officers and men of 42 Commando, Royal Marines, the Welsh Guards, and HMS *Invincible* for the kindness they showed us throughout the campaign. We would also like to express our gratitude to our editors, Charles Douglas-Home of *The Times* and Donald Trelford, of the *Observer*, for generously allowing us time to write this book, and to John Shirley of the *Sunday Times* and Robert Fox of the BBC for their advice.

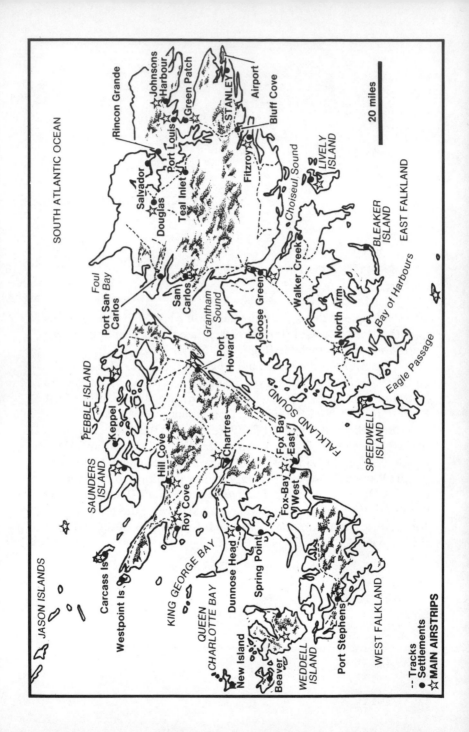

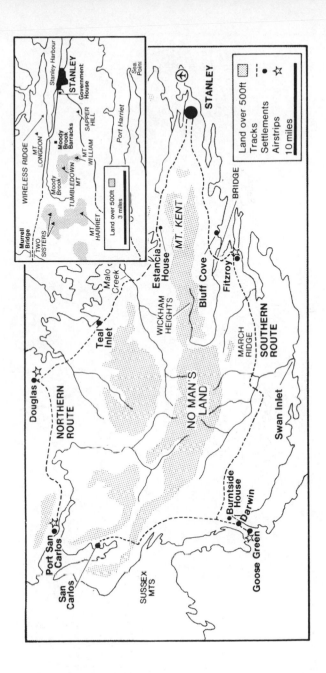

Prologue:

One Small War

It was a while before anyone realized that the guns had stopped firing. We were standing on a rock ledge on the east face of Mount Harriet looking down towards the town. The crags around were chipped and smashed by the fighting of the last two days and the pathetic debris of the Argentinian defenders lay strewn all around. At three o'clock we heard some uncertain cheers from the Marines on the rocks above. 'That's it,' one of them shouted. 'They've surrendered.' One of the officers, Major Mike Norman, who had been captured and sent back to England by the Argentine invaders ten weeks before, laughed and shook hands with an officer standing next to him, but the rest of us wanted the news to be true too badly to rejoice until we were sure.

The commanding officer, Colonel Vaux, went over to the radio and called up Brigade. 'It's not confirmed,' he said. 'It's just something they got from fleet.' It started to snow again. Colonel Vaux went back to the radio. 'They're falling back from Sapper Hill!' he said. 'There are white arm bands and flags all over the place.'

The same news was travelling fast across the battlefield. The Welsh Guards scarcely had time to take it in before being ordered forward to Sapper Hill, the last Argentine stronghold before Port Stanley. Tired soldiers staggered out of their 'bashers' pulling kit

13

into rucksacks and piled into Sea King and Wessex helicopters to be ferried the last few kilometres to the foot of the hill. Inside the aircraft the soldiers gave each other nervous grins. The elation at the news that the Argentinians were retreating had been replaced by uncertainty as to whether they were flying to witness a surrender or to fight the final battle. The helicopters shuddered to the ground by a jagged outcrop of rock on an unmetalled road running by the side of Mount William. The men jumped out and scrambled into the heather looking for cover. There were no Argentinians in view. 'Get back on the road, those surrounds are mined,' shouted an officer.

The men returned to the track and set off towards the outline of Sapper Hill. Their faces were dark with camouflage cream and tiredness but the pace as they walked got faster and faster. The intelligence officer, Captain Piers Minoprio, was called to the radio. 'There's a white flag over Stanley,' he shouted. We were trotting down the road now, passing soldiers struggling along with enormous packs and heavy machine guns. The order came down the line to 'close up' and 'unfix bayonets'. The defenders' abandoned possessions littered the sides of the road: kit bags, blankets and helmets. Mud-stained comic books and letters from home skipped about in the wind. We passed an artillery position still smoking from the battering it had received from the British guns. The ground around it was churned up like a newly ploughed field. Two Marines were lying by the side of the road. One had a dark red patch spreading across his trouser leg and the other had a bloody blotch on his head. Medical orderlies were hunched over them murmuring reassurance. We climbed on to a Scorpion tank and caught up with the forward Commandos who were skirting the base of Sapper Hill. They had been fired on by the retreating Argentinians as they ran out of their helicopter and there had been a firefight that lasted twenty minutes. It was probably the last skirmish of the war.

A sergeant showed us an ammunition pouch in his fighting order that had been hit by a bullet and exploded. We rounded the bend and came within sight of Stanley. An Argentine corpse was lying face down in the middle of the road. The soldiers peered at the body, full of curiosity. 'Spread out lads!' shouted one of the NCOs. 'Take care, this is too easy.' The troops moved up the muddy path on to Sapper Hill, scouring the ground in front of their feet for signs of mines. We knew the name of the hill well from numerous intelligence briefings and it had been the Guards' objective in the renewed assault due to take place that night, but now the machine gun positions and trenches were empty. A vehicle lay abandoned at the side of the road and there were ration tins and biscuits trodden into the mud around the dug-outs. The only sound was the wind and the tramp of boots. Down below in Stanley, smoke swirled away from shelled houses. The Argentine soldiers stood by their dug-outs staring in our direction. The capital looked suburban and insubstantial in the watery light, a smattering of green- and red-roofed houses. The large red cross on the roof of the hospital stood out in the middle of the town. A white helicopter buzzed across the bay carrying casualties to the Argentine hospital ship *Bahia Paraiso*. The Welsh Guards' commanding officer, Lt.-Col Johnny Rickett, stood on the crest of the hill taking a swig from a whisky bottle that was passing among the officers. Brigadier Tony Wilson, the commander of the 5th Infantry Brigade, joined him looking down on the town. 'It seems an incredibly long way to come for this,' he said.

The troops were told to wait outside Stanley while negotiations were started for a surrender, so we decided to go in ahead of them. We stripped off our camouflage kit, piling it next to one of the 155mm guns that had been shelling us the night before, and started to walk the last half mile into town. It was difficult to know what attitude to strike with the Argentine soldiers who sat by the road in trenches pointing their guns towards us. We tried to be as ostentatiously harmless as possible, waving and calling greetings, but there was no response and it was hard to stop speculating about how it might feel to be struck by a bullet. As we reached a cattle-grid on the edge of town three Argentine conscripts approached. They were unarmed and grinning and insisted on shaking our hands. For the first time we felt that the battle for the Falklands was all but over.

The speed of the Argentinian collapse that Monday morning astounded everybody. The British had been appealing to them to surrender for four days without receiving any sign that they were prepared to do so and most of the soldiers were expecting to fight through Stanley street by street. Just as the news of the surrender came through, the commander of the land forces on the Falkland Islands, Maj.-Gen. Jeremy Moore, had just ordered an air raid on Sapper Hill to blast the Argentinians with cluster bombs. 'I heard on the radio that the Argentine soldiers were all walking about and I had a Harrier strike due to go in,' he said. 'I grabbed the radio myself and did all the talking for the next two hours. The strike was due within minutes and if it had gone ahead it may have meant the whole war continuing.'

Considering the war ended in a reasonably neat and satisfying way for Britain it is easy to forget that it began in muddle and semi-farce. Ostensibly it started on 18 March 1982, when Constantine Sergio Davidoff, a Greek Argentine scrap metal merchant with a contract to dismember an old whaling station on South Georgia ran up the blue and white Argentinian flag to remind the world of Argentina's claim to the territory, which had been acquired by Britain at the beginning of the century. It took time for the consequences of this small *coup de théâtre* to develop. When diplomatic representations met with calculated indifference in Buenos Aires it became clear that Davidoff's action was a deliberate test of Britain's will. Up until then the dispute over the ownership of the Falklands had, in the eyes of Britain at least, shown a capacity to be stretched, painlessly, into infinity. But on 2 April, a day late it was said to exploit the full irony of the situation, Argentina invaded the Falklands, expelled the British garrison of Royal Marines and declared them the Islas Malvinas. Britain reacted first with indignation and then with force.

Even when the task force set sail it was hard to take the business too seriously. 'See you in a week,' said one of our editors as preparations were made to join the fleet at Portsmouth. The predominant feeling during the first few days at sea was that this show of might was a faintly ludicrous reaction to a dispute that would almost certainly be resolved by diplomatic means. The Argentinians would soon realize the extent of their effrontery and their isolation from the rest of world opinion, and withdraw.

We comforted ourselves with the thought of the size of the diplomatic machinery that was available to shift the protagonists off a collision course before the crash happened and there was, it appeared, plenty of time. The newspapers seemed confident that if it did come to a fight the odds were almost embarrassingly unfair. It was a contest, they said, between the first and the third division. In this buoyant atmosphere some of the soldiers felt that the worst outcome would be if a diplomatic solution was arrived at before a shot was fired and we all had to turn round and come home. The Navy were more cautious. At least the soldiers had some idea of what sort of conflict they might be going into. The Navy had never been in a missile war and had a healthy fear of the horrors it might involve.

The Falklands campaign had many of the characteristics of a nineteenth-century military encounter. It was in essence an old-fashioned punitive expedition and the cause of the dispute concerned territory not ideology. It was a short war with a beginning, a middle and an end. Apart from the missiles, modern technology played a minor part and the basic weapons would have been familiar to any veteran of World War II. It was a clean war. Both sides abided by the rules and if there were any atrocities they have not yet come to light. Most of all it was, unusually for the twentieth century, a remarkably two-sided war. Both sides had to rely, fundamentally, on their own soldiery and stocks of weapons without any decisive military assistance from an outside power.

The British could reasonably claim to have done almost everything for themselves. They took a pride in their ability to mount such an operation, at such a distance, at a time of economic feebleness and national self-doubt that will probably look excessive in years to come. The Argentinians, in defeat, claimed that it was American aid and economic sanctions that finished them. The first part at least is untrue. In the military side of the drama the Americans had scarcely a walk-on part. Even the accounts of the war were two-sided. The press corps of thirty journalists who travelled with the task force was exclusively British. For once the ubiquitous camera crews of NBC and CBS were absent and the world was forced to watch events unfold through the eyes of the two protagonists.

A few hours before the Welsh Guards were due to start an attack on a force of 250 Argentinians dug in below Mount William, one of their officers was asked what the strategy was for the action. 'We'll sneak up on them, open fire and give them cold steel up their arse,' he replied. Every newcomer to the battlefield was struck at what a primitive business it was. Tactics seemed to have changed little from the last war or indeed the Great War. The basic tools for fighting were artillery, mortars, machine guns and bayonets. Several of the mountain-top battles ended with the British soldiers lunging at the departing backs with steel. Because the Argentine tanks and armoured vehicles played no part in the fighting, many of the more modern weapons were never used for their original purpose. The Paras' 'Wombat' anti-tank guns stayed on the ships and the Milan wire-guided missiles were used almost exclusively and with horrific effect for firing into Argentinian bunkers.

The anti-aircraft missiles were employed with mixed results. The Blowpipes, under suspicion from the outset, turned out to be cumbersome and to miss the jets with depressing frequency, although they were more successful against the piston-engined Pucaras that hopped around the islands terrifying the helicopter pilots. Naval visitors to the battlefield were surprised to see that so much of it was still a matter of trenches and artillery bombardments and that the first thing you did when you stopped was to start digging a hole. The battle on Mount Longdon proved that a single sniper could still hold up a company of men. The planes were fast and sophisticated but they could still be brought down by small-arms fire. The well-tried tactics of military warfare were the ones that succeeded; diversionary raids, surprise attacks and night operations. This approach also had the benefit of keeping down the number of casualties. The British equipment was no better than the Argentinians'. In some cases it was the same, but unlike the Argentinians, the British looked after it. The troops kept up the habit of stripping and cleaning their self-loading rifles, even on top of the mountains, so that at the end of the campaign they were oiled and spotless in comparison to the rusting and battered piles of weaponry left behind by the Argentinians. Despite the helicopters and the Volvo tracked vehicles it was a war where most of the troops marched to the front. 3 Para walked all the way from Port San Carlos to Port Stanley. The ability to move long distances loaded up with equipment and weapons was something the Argentinians had not accounted for and part of their reasoning for not attacking the beach-head at San Carlos at the beginning of the landing appears to have been because they believed that the task force would soon get bogged down and fall vulnerable to the Argentinian Air Force.

The marches were forced on the troops by the shortage of helicopters but they took a masochistic pleasure in the ordeal. It was not any great belief in the justice of the cause that propelled them along. Most of the argument about the rights and wrongs of the affair had ended a few weeks before the landing. If anything, the case for going to war over the Falklands diminished rather than grew the more you saw of the place and its inhabitants. Mostly it was pride in themselves and their organizations that motivated them. Many of the men were from Britain's economic wastelands: the Clyde, Ulster, the North-East, and they had better experience than anyone else in the country of its imperfections and injustices. They joined up in many cases because there was nothing else to do. The war was not won on the playing fields of Eton but on the tarmac playground of a Glasgow comprehensive. The soldiers showed an extraordinary capacity for pain and discomfort. By the time they arrived in Port Stanley many of them had spent seventeen days in the open. That meant an existence of continual dirt, wet and cold. It was not always necessary for them to have been quite so uncomfortable. We sometimes asked why the soldiers did not carry tents, which seemed much more sensible and less time-consuming than the usual business of building a shelter out of a waterproof poncho and bits of string, but no one ever had a convincing explanation. We got the impression that tents were somehow regarded as 'sissy'. In the last days of the war, when the task force commanders began to get worried about the state of the troops on the mountains, some tents were found and sent up to them.

The soldiers met all these privations with an uncomplaining acceptance which seemed almost unnatural. Their reaction to the horrors of the campaign was usually to make a joke and laugh. At one level this was simply a case of laughing because otherwise you might cry; humour was the balm of tragedy. The Welsh Guardsmen who staggered ashore from the *Galahad*, blackened and shocked, spent their first moments on the beach joking about what had happened. A motorcycle messenger in the Welsh Guards was killed when he ran his bike over a mine after bringing rations up to the front line. 'At least he copped it on the way back,' someone said.

This flip callousness was a feature of most of the humour. Brigadier Julian Thompson, commanding officer of 3 Commando brigade, said the funniest moment of the war for him was watching an officer caught in a small boat in San Carlos Water during the middle of a bombing raid. The outboard engine had broken down and he was paddling frantically to get ashore. People were unsentimental about the dead, at least during the time the fighting was going on. The death of Colonel 'H.' Jones, commanding officer of 2 Para, who was undoubtedly popular, even loved by a lot of the soldiers, produced only formal expressions of regret when the news came through that he had been killed.

For all that, the soldiers were not unfeeling people. The military operated an 'oppo' system where each soldier had a best friend upon whom he could rely and who would look after him in turn when necessary. The system worked. In battle the men risked their own lives to patch up their wounded friends and carry them back to the regimental aid post. They sometimes got horribly injured doing so. Two Scots Guards had their feet blown off carrying their injured 'oppos' out of a minefield.

On the whole they treated the Argentine soldiers well too, and despite there being plenty of opportunities, there were no orgies of killing. Apart from the odd bout of verbal abuse they left the prisoners alone and for the most part were objects of contemptuous curiosity. After the victory there was much talk about how well the Argentinians had fought but most of the soldiers had a fairly low opinion of the soldiering abilities of their opponents. 'Military pygmies,' was how one SAS officer described them. Some of the British troops had a tendency to ghoulishness. A seventeen-year-old Argentinian conscript who was shot through the mouth during the battle for Mount Harriet and buried where he fell was dug up by a 'bootie' who wanted to photograph him for his album.

It is extraordinary the extent to which people behave in a war in the way that the war films would have you believe. In the middle of the battle for Mount Tumbledown we saw a young Guards lieutenant from the Blues and Royals wandering down the road from the fighting looking fiercely indignant. 'The swine have gone and blown up my tank,' he said. Earlier on, while wandering around in the darkness in the worst weather of the war looking for a trench, we came across a lone figure hunched against the wind, his cape flowing behind him like a Superman cartoon. 'Who was that outside?' we asked when we found some shelter. 'Oh, that will be Lord Dalrymple,' said a sergeant. 'He's always out there.' On the day after the battle for Mount Longdon a pair of Harriers swooped along the side of Mount Kent on their way to a bombing raid on Port Stanley and as the troops cheered and shouted they switched on their vapour trails and climbed into the sky leaving a perfect victory 'V' in their wake.

People spoke in war comic clichés. They really did say, 'We're going to knock the Argies for six.' A Marine lieutenant heading off on a night patrol to draw the enemy fire and locate their positions said: 'Looks like we're set for some good sport tonight.' Perhaps because it had been so long since Britain had fought a conventional war a lot of the language and images were borrowed from American literature and films about the Vietnam war. 'It's just like *Apocalypse Now*,' said a Marine in awe watching the tracer crackle over the side of Mount Harriet. Soldiers predicted that if the Argies were 'zapped' heavily enough they were bound to 'bug out'.

The doctors and medical orderlies in the gloomy field dressing station at Ajax Bay and on board the hospital ship *Uganda* half consciously modelled themselves on the heroes of 'MASH' although the best words and expressions were their own. 'Yomping' was an almost onomatopoeiac term for trekking heavily-laden over difficult ground. It described the activity perfectly. No one knew where it came from, though exhaustive research by John Silverlight of the *Observer* seems to suggest it has its origins in the Norwegian skiing term for crossing an obstacle.

Significantly, there were two terms for acquiring pieces of equipment dishonestly. One was called 'proffing', the other 'rassing', derived from the naval shorthand for Replenishment At Sea. Looted items were known as 'gizzits', short for 'give us it'. 'Proffing' was a way of life. One of us left a pair of ski gloves to dry out on top of a boiler in a settlement farmhouse and within half an hour they were gone. A little later a Guardsman walked by wearing them. He swore he had found them elsewhere and already his name was inscribed across the back in large black letters. Some of the most sought-after articles were the waterproof overboots that were much prized as a means of preventing trench foot. To take them off and leave them unattended was taken as an indication that you no longer had any further use for them. Courage was measured in two ways. First there was the extent of your ability to 'hack it'; to keep going in adverse conditions. That you failed to hack it was almost the worst thing that could be said of you. Second there was the size and quality of your 'bottle'. This was really old-fashioned daring. People who charged machine gun posts armed only with a fixed bayonet had a 'lot of bottle'. That you 'bottled out' was definitely the worst thing that could be said of you. The most useful military word was 'kit'. The military applied it to everything from a compo-ration tin-opener to a Hercules transport plane. This could be carried to extremes though. We heard one officer referring to his girlfriend as 'a good bit of kit'.

When it came to the nastier side of their trade the military tended to go in for euphemisms. Apart from the SAS who invariably used direct terminology, you rarely heard people talk about killing Argentinians. They 'took them out', 'wasted' them or 'blew them away'. Troops were never shelled. They were 'malleted', 'banjoed' or 'brassed up'. It did not sound too alarming to hear over the ship's tannoy that there was some 'air activity' thirty miles away until you realized that it meant some Argentine aircraft were on their way over to try and bomb you. To make the experience less harrowing the incoming raiders were often called 'dago airways' in the running commentaries that went on during the attacks on *Fearless*. 'We have some good news and some bad news,' said a naval officer over the tannoy one day. 'The good news is that four Argentinian aircraft are approaching from the west presenting excellent targets for our Harriers and missiles. The bad news is that they are Super Etendards carrying Exocet.' Nothing was known by its real name. Food was 'scran' or 'scoff'. The sea was the 'oggin' and our cabins were 'pits' or 'grots'.

One of the reasons all this terminology sounded so odd was that the military was a foreign country to most of us. Because the days of national service were long gone few of the journalists knew what sort of men they were and how the Army operated. Having worked in Northern Ireland was not much of a help as it has been recent government policy to shield the Army from publicity and to prevent the emergence of any military 'personalities', so that few people can now tell you who the officer is commanding forces there. In the absence of a conventional conflict for so long, the picture the public has of the upper reaches of the military has grown so faint as to be almost invisible. The heads of the services who sprung to prominence during the conflict were unknown men to most people. Brigadiers Thompson and Wilson, for example, do not even appear in *Who's Who*.

In view of this lack of information we tended to make crude assumptions about what these men would be like. Few of them matched the stereotypes. There was something Victorian about many of them. Most of the battalion commanders had been educated at the better-known public schools and gone straight into the Army. The Para and Marine commanding officers tended to be practical, spartan men who shared all the discomforts their men had to put up with. We were surprised when we went ashore to see 42 Commando's CO, Lt.-Col Vaux, carrying a pack not much smaller than those of the 'booties' around him.

Although the officers shared the lives of the men and a close relationship grew up between them, at the end of the day they were still separated by an almost unbridgeable divide. Officers might call the subordinates by their Christian names when they were on their own together but it would never happen in public. The officers joined the forces as a career, the men as a job. The great majority of the soldiers knew when they joined up that they were in the ranks for the duration of their army lives, and for most of them it did not matter. To make the leap from the ranks meant taking examinations, including a knives and forks test to gauge your suitability for the rigours of the officers' mess. 'There are occasions when it is permissible, almost desirable, to throw a pint of beer over your neighbour's head at dinner,' a Marine lieutenant explained. 'There are other times when it is not.' The Parachute Regiment was the keenest to commission good NCOs and at least three majors in the campaign had joined the Army as privates.

We knew little about the men at the top of the chain of command, for Admiral Sir John Fieldhouse, Commander-in-Chief Fleet, ran the war from the Navy's operations' headquarters, an underground bunker at Northwood, in north-west London. The task force commander was Rear Admiral John Woodward, who was based throughout the war on HMS *Hermes*, the older of the two aircraft carriers with the fleet. He was called 'Sandy' because of his reddish hair and was the *primus inter pares* among the task force commanders. Both he and General Moore answered to Fieldhouse, but although Moore was in charge of the land forces, the local operation came under Woodward's control. He was a retiring man, who played chess and solved mathematical problems as a hobby. Early on in the campaign his methods started to draw criticism from the Army. Most of it stemmed from Woodward's preoccupation with the air and sea war and his determination to keep the losses of the fleet to a minimum. His nickname among some members of the land forces, and indeed some of the Navy too who were on the ships in San Carlos Water taking a daily battering from the Argentine jets, was 'Windy Woodward' and he was awarded the 'Burma Star' for keeping the carriers so far east. It is hard to see what other course was open to him. For the British to win the war it was vital for them to have aeroplanes and if one or the other of the carriers was sunk the war would almost certainly have been at an end. Woodward's first obligation was to keep *Hermes* and *Invincible* and the Harriers they carried safe, but by doing so he won few friends.

In some ways Woodward personified the Navy's aloofness compared with the more relaxed attitude of the Army, and its gaucheness in dealing with the press. Northern Ireland had taught the Marines and Paras the power of publicity. The Navy, on the other hand, rarely came across the media, except perhaps once a year when the local television station turned up to film the gun race. Soon after the taking of South Georgia Woodward told the reporters on *Hermes* that the task force was now ready for the 'heavy punch' against the invaders and issued a public warning to the Argentinians. 'If you want to get out I suggest you do so now,' he said. 'Once we arrive the only way home will be by courtesy of the Royal Navy.' This was rousing quotable stuff and it quickly earned him a rebuke from Northwood for appearing too belligerent. A meeting with him a few days after the incident gave the impression of a nice, slightly naïve man. 'I don't regard myself as the hawk-eyed, sharp-nosed hard military man leading a battle fleet into the annals of history,' he said. 'I am very astonished to find myself in this position. I am an ordinary person who lives in southwest London in suburbia and I have been a virtual civil servant for the past three years commuting into London every day.' Whether this peace-mongering appeased Northwood we never learnt but after that Woodward stopped talking to the press.

Maj.-Gen. Jeremy Moore was a small, lean man who bristled with energy. He was the Marines' most decorated serving officer, having won a Military Cross in Malaya in 1950 and a bar twelve years later for commanding an amphibious assault against some rebels in Brunei. Moore led a company of Marines in two small river boats in a surprise attack on 350 rebels who were holding some British civilians hostage. They killed scores of them, lost five men themselves and rescued the prisoners. He was awarded an OBE for his part in Operation Motorman which ended the no-go areas in Northern Ireland. Moore was a religious man and liked to quote from Bonhoeffer as well as von Clausewitz. He was reputed to carry a Bible in his breast pocket. He liked to get around the battlefield and regularly flew up the mountains to check on the progress of the war from the front line, wandering around in a khaki forage cap and a kit bag with 'Moore' on the back. The lack of insignia on his uniform added to his air of authority. His role in the war was that of a logistician and administrator. He came out to the Falklands to act as a buffer between Woodward and Thompson and their masters in London and to smooth relations between the land force and the fleet. He said afterwards: 'I had to take the political pressure off Julian's back. He was involved in constant referring upwards to all levels in London and the fleet. It was his job to concentrate on the build-up for the attack on Stanley.'

Julian Thompson was the most obviously intelligent of the commanders; quotable, brisk and amusing. Despite leading a faultless campaign, he claimed not to have derived much pleasure from it. Sitting in his office in Port Stanley, he said: 'I'm always reminded of the saying of Robert E. Lee. "It is a good thing that war is so terrible otherwise we would enjoy it too much."' Among the half-dozen recurring military maxims of the campaign, this was one of the favourites. Thompson was the commander with the most claim to be the architect of the victory. It was his plan. He chose the landing site and the route that the troops would follow to Stanley, aided all along by the SAS and SBS teams who were helicoptered on to the islands on 1 May to reconnoitre around Port Stanley, San Carlos, Goose Green and Port Howard. It was a conventional plan but it had its subtleties and it worked.

Rivalry between the components of the task force was endemic. It started at the very bottom of the military structure, with one platoon speaking disparagingly about the abilities of another, and spread upwards. One battalion in a regiment would try and outdo the other. At various points the rivals would come together against a common 'enemy' so that the Marines on occasion formed a united front against the Paras and in turn the whole of 3 Commando Brigade looked down slightly on the Guards and Gurkhas, maintaining they were more professional. At the top of the structure the Army would join forces occasionally to snipe at the Navy. The one thing everybody agreed on was that the RAF had not distinguished themselves. The Vulcan bombing raids, when only one of sixty-three bombs hit the runway at Stanley airfield, provoked widespread hilarity.

When the war was over General Moore, inevitably quoting another soldier, said it had been 'a close run thing'. When the fleet set sail it seemed impossible the Argentinians could win. After it was over it was difficult to see how they had lost. Their weapons were just as good as those of the British and better in some cases. They had two months to prepare their defences and at the start of the war they outnumbered their attackers by three to one, a direct inversion of the odds that conventional military wisdom dictates. They had nothing like the logistical problems that beset their attackers and right to the end they were getting nightly visits from C130 transport planes flying in from the mainland. The myth of starving and disease-ridden Argentine conscripts was one that rankled with task force troops when they discovered that the defenders were in fact rather better fed than they were. The mistake was letting the British establish a beach-head in the first place. In some ways the Argentinians were justified in thinking that their Air Force could drive the British back before the invasion took root. If the French had supplied more Exocets, if more of the bombs they dropped had exploded, then the course of the war could have changed utterly. The losses that the British did sustain shook the task force commanders. If every bomb which hit a ship on D Day had exploded, the momentum of the campaign would have been stalled and the return to diplomacy would have seemed the only option. The Argentinians never solved the problem of the unexploded bombs. The Navy's view was that the fuses were set for one height but the Argentine pilots were dropping them at another, coming in too low to 'arm' them in an attempt to get underneath the canopy of missiles and small-arms fire that the fleet put up whenever the raiders appeared. If the fuses had been shorter, however, the pilots would have run the risk of blasting their own planes out of the sky.

Once the British were ashore, the Argentinians had a rack of natural defences stretching all the way from the beach-head back to Port Stanley which, if properly fortified and defended, could have held up the advance for months. Yet they chose to give away almost all the ground up to the gates of Stanley. Mount Kent, which dominates the east end of the island, was given up without a fight. When the Argentinians chose to make a stand they often ignored elementary rules of infantry combat. They poured resources into Mount Longdon but neglected to push out advance patrols or train artillery in front of the stronghold so that the Paras were able to move up to their positions unimpeded. Both the Argentinian and the British commanders said that in the end it was the destructive power of the British which forced the surrender: the thirty 105mm field pieces and the rapid-firing 4.5inch naval guns that rained shells on the capital and the defensive perimeter during the last days of the fighting. But by that stage the war was nearly over. The fundamental difference between the two sides was the quality of the infantry men. The paratroopers' victory at Goose Green over an enemy three times as numerous took place with minimal artillery support and against a heavy and skilful Argentine bombardment. In the end the Argentinians were disinclined to fight even though their soldiers probably felt the justice of their cause as much as their attackers did. The bulk of the Army was conscripted, and when the shooting started the NCOs were incapable of keeping their men in the trenches. After Goose Green, and as the British moved closer and closer, they seemed to have been overtaken by a creeping fatalism. Looking down from Mount Longdon the officer commanding A Company of 3 Para reported: 'For the company the following two days provided some "good sport". Having become established on the feature we found ourselves almost in the middle of the enemy camp, being able to observe and bring down harassing fire on all the main enemy positions. The two company MFCs, Corporals Crowne and Baxter, called it an MFC's dream. The enemy seemed to show little concern for this harassing fire, and even continued to drive to and from Moody Brook and Stanley at night with headlights when meeting the nightly C130 flights. The number of targets was so great that they could not all be engaged.'

The British, on the other hand, had troops that were not only trained to perfection for just such a war as this but also had a pride in their abilities and a degree of determination that made the prospect of defeat almost intolerable. George Orwell wrote in *Homage to Catalonia*: 'People forget that a soldier anywhere near the front line is usually too hungry or frightened or cold or above all too tired to care about the political origins of the war.' The British were no idealogues. They were just better soldiers.

It has not taken long for the memories of the Falklands war to dim. The things that are still vivid are the noises: the perpetual wop-wop of helicopters, the buzz of artillery shells. Neither of us had been shelled before. Like everything in the war it was surprising how quickly you adapted to it though no one ever got used to it.

We were only fired on for a few hours but we soon learned to distinguish between the whizz of outgoing fire and the whistle of incoming. We experienced brief moments of terror but knew that if we were properly dug in it would take a direct hit to kill us, although this was rumoured to have happened to one unlucky man who had his head knocked off by a shell. 'His number was definitely on that one,' the teller would invariably say, whenever the story was repeated. The smells are still easy to recall: the hot eye-watering blast of aviation spirit exhaust that hit you every time you got on and off a helicopter. The powdery tang of artillery smoke and the acrid smell of a hexamine fuel block. There are other ineradicable memories: the horrible stillness of dead bodies; the sight of a row of survivors from *Ardent*, their expressionless faces smeared a ghastly white with flamazime anti-burn cream, lying on the floor of the

Ajax Bay field dressing station.

The war was a profound experience but not a particularly revealing one. On the whole it tended to confirm the truth of clichés. It did bring out the best in people: courage in the case of the civilian crews of the troop ships who more than anyone had the right to wonder what on earth they were doing there; compassion and dedication in the doctors and nurses who tended the casualties.

And at times it was hellish. The nights were long, about fourteen hours of darkness in which there was nothing to do but sleep, for we were not allowed to show any lights after dusk in case we gave away our position. It was always numbingly cold. We lived with seven layers of clothing on our chests and three on our legs and slept in them all, and usually with our boots on too. But despite the cold and the wet and the uncertainty, like everyone in this winter war we always slept well.

1

The Empire Strikes Back

HMS *Invincible* edged away from the quayside shortly before 10 a.m. on Monday, 5 April, tugs and small chase boats buzzing around her like impatient flies. She moved grandly down the Portsmouth Channel, exchanging salutes with ships and acknowledging the cheers of thousands of people lining the rooftops, quays and beaches in the crisp spring sunshine. Union flags skipped and curled above blurred heads and caps were doffed in extravagant gestures. From the Admiral's bridge we could see the lone Sea Harrier fixed to the 'ski jump', its nose pointing skywards. At the stern helicopters squatted on the flight deck, their blades strapped back like broken insects. The order for *Invincible*'s Attention' to the 500 men lining the deck in their best rig was swept away by the wind and they 'came to' like a group of conscripts on their first day's drill. We moved away from the small boats, past the old sea forts and into the Channel. Behind us came HMS *Hermes*, the old warhorse, already looking stained and weatherbeaten. A small group of men, for once not caught up in the urgency of departure, stood staring back at 'Pompey', others gazed towards the horizon. It had been a long time since the country sailed to war.

The speed of developments since Argentina invaded the Falklands three days earlier had been breathtaking. Crewmen, called back at short notice from their winter sports, had clambered aboard carrying skis while others arrived with rucksacks from hiking holidays. Every available Sea Harrier had been grabbed and warehouses emptied of spares and food.

The departure, however, gave the men a chance to collect their thoughts. There was a slight sense of the absurd; of a Gilbert and Sullivan operetta with the might of the Royal Navy off to bloody the noses of a bunch of bean-eaters. But the tears in the eyes of the young man on the bridge were real enough and there was no doubt on board that we had to avenge a wrong and restore national pride. Alongside pictures of the ships in the task force someone had put up a notice: 'The Empire Strikes Back'.

But would it come to a fight? We were confident we were off on a cruise, a piece of sabre-rattling to concentrate General Galtieri's mind and hasten a diplomatic solution. The days of gunboat diplomacy were over and surely no one would be foolish enough to fight over some far-flung islands at the bottom of the world? Not everyone on board, however, was so convinced. Captain Jeremy Black said on the second day, while we were still within sight of land, that war was likely. He had to say this to prepare the crew for the worst, but he also identified the issue of sovereignty over the islands as the major stumbling block to a peaceful settlement. In the end he was proved right.

Gradually the rather jolly outing began to appear less jolly and hearing a rating sing 'Don't cry for me Argentina', lost its charm. The only two board games in the wardroom were Risk and Diplomacy. The latter was rarely played. Even the notice in the flying room which said 'Due to the untimely death of Mae West all life preservers will be known as Dolly Partons', became less amusing. We were simply more concerned with getting a life jacket. As the mood of the ship darkened the closer we moved to the Falklands, so the British bulldog spirit of affronted pride gave way to a greater degree of realism and apprehension.

The officers, and especially the pilots, though, remained pugnacious throughout. 'I've been dying for ages to have a limited war,' commented Lt.-Com. 'Sharky' Ward. 'It enables us to sort out the chaff and cut through the red tape.' A helicopter pilot, Lieutenant Darryl Whitehead, married two days before we sailed and who might be expected to have other things on his mind, added in a surprising aside: 'I know it sounds a bit bloodthirsty, but I would like to drop a real depth charge on a real target.'

The ratings demonstrated a more understandable desire to stay alive. Officers would speak of them getting 'the jitters on the lower decks' and at times they looked distinctly nervous. The crew were careful to express their doubts out of earshot of the officers. On a visit to the frigate, HMS *Broadsword*, we asked junior ratings in their tiny mess in the bowels of the ship, 'What do you think of it so far?' 'Rubbish,' came the stock reply. 'Do you want to go home?' 'Not 'alf,' they said, more seriously. An officer stuck his head round the door. 'Do you think we ought to kick the Argies off the Falklands, lads?' he enquired encouragingly. 'Yeah, they orta be taught a lesson,' was the response. As we filed from the room one of the boys, no older than eighteen, winked.

But however nervous we became at times, the men were touched by that Portsmouth send-off and the mass of mail and the young girls demanding to be pen pals. They knew the country was united behind them and their tattoos 'Made in Britain' (or 'Brewed in Essex' on their beer guts) displayed their nationalism.

The pulse of the ship was taken daily by the Captain, like a caring family GP. Much later in the voyage, after the *Belgrano* and *Sheffield* were sunk, the question of morale was raised when he doubted the veracity of two pieces we had written. One hack had seen a rating sitting on the floor during the threat of an Exocet attack, tears rolling down his cheeks as he looked at a picture of his girlfriend, and another had told me that until Argentina fired that first missile all he knew about the country was that they ate corned beef and played football. Now he rated them. The captain found it hard to believe his men could behave or speak in such a way. In the cramped confines of a ship, where men lived cheek by jowl for months on end, discipline was essential; especially during a push-button war where seconds matter – 'the land of the quick or the dead'. By writing about the crew's doubts the Captain thought discipline and morale would be undermined. One thousand men were crammed together on *Invincible*, from Prince Andrew, then second in line to the throne, to the lowliest rating from the Gorbals. Although there was interplay between the different ranks, their boundaries were jealously guarded. Most preferred it that way. Morale was certainly mercurial. It could ebb and flow according to ship 'buzzes', the internal word-of-mouth system that got messages around almost as fast as the tannoy. It was widely believed, for instance, there would be R and R (rest and recreation) at Mombasa then Rio de Janeiro. Spirits soared. When the speciousness of these rumours was exposed they plummeted. Such buzzes frequently seemed to originate from the cooks' galley, inhabited by large red-faced chefs who dreamed up mischief as they stirred their pots.

As the task force moved south, Operation Corporate, as it was now known, became increasingly secretive. Naval ships with their supply vessels had been leaving Britain and Gibraltar over a period of days bound for the rendezvous point at Ascension Island. Radio silence was observed and vessels were darkened at night. The crew was told it could not mention the ship's position, speed and accompanying vessels in letters home. *Invincible*, in fact, was travelling south on only one propeller at about fifteen knots. Almost as soon as we left Portsmouth one of the gear couplings of the giant engines had shattered and teams of engineers worked round the clock for two weeks to replace it by the time we reached Ascension. It was a remarkable effort that went unreported due to the Navy's desire to keep everything from the Argentinians that could prove useful. For the first few days we hardly caught a glimpse of any other ships and we imagined a lonely voyage for 8,000 miles with empty horizons. Then *Hermes* moved closer and for the remainder of the journey we could see at least four or five vessels, their dull, grey shapes discernible against the sky. It was not quite like scenes from *The Cruel Sea*, with warships hammering along with only a few cables between them, but it was oddly reassuring.

The secrecy reflected not only the Navy's obsession with stealth but also the growing state of readiness for war. Harriers were flying more or less continually; rocketing a 'splash target' dragged behind the ship, firing a Sidewinder heat-seeking missile at a phosphorus flare, dropping bombs and feigning attacks on other ships to test their responses. Sea King helicopters flew endless missions, probing the oceans with their active sonars like huge insects dipping their probosces into the sea. They would look for unidentified shipping, throwing the £5m. machine around the sky like a piece of paper caught in the wind. Besides searching for hostile submarines they acted as scouts for missile-carrying ships, doing 'over the horizon targeting' which involved popping up for a look and then getting out of radar contact, very fast. I was just recovering from a bout of sea-sickness in the Bay of Biscay (the first and last time) and could scarcely take my eyes off a fixed point three feet in front of me as the helicopter dropped from 400 feet to just above the waves in seconds. They had a favourite trick of allowing a guest to take the controls and then switching off the stabilizer. The aircraft would plunge wildly before the co-pilot took over. Outings would turn into sing-songs, with the four-man crew going through 820 Squadron's repertory over their internal radios. Every flight ended with a return to 'mother', the pilots' term for *Invincible* that Freud would have loved. The helicopter crewmen tended to be younger than the Harrier pilots, many of whom were in their mid-thirties and had years of experience flying Buccaneers and Phantom jets. The Sea King crews were wilder, liable to stand round the wardroom piano singing lewd songs, play fearsome games and crawl to bed.

One of the junior pilots was Sub-Lieutenant Prince Andrew, who had joined 820 Ringbolt Squadron (motto: Shield and Avenge) the previous October. The other pilots were fiercely protective, thinking it poor form to talk about him behind his back. The most one of his friends would say was that he had improved since his training days at Dartmouth when he had appeared rather standoffish. At first he had avoided the journalists in the wardroom, obviously slightly ill-at-ease with having the press at such close proximity, especially newspapers like the *Sun* and *Daily Star* which had hardly endeared themselves to the Royal family. We had been told not to make the first move and after a while he approached us, curious about the working of the press and telling us how he had evaded the *paparazzi* with tricks 'the length of his arm', none of which he would disclose. Another of his friends said he actually liked appearing in the papers, and became slightly irritated if there was no photograph or harmless story about 'Randy Andy'.

For a twenty-two-year-old he was a curious mixture of maturity and youth. His voice and mannerisms were strikingly similar to those of Prince Charles, although his sense of humour, always just below the surface, was more direct than Charles's satirical approach. One one occasion he took great delight in telling the man from the *Sun* that he relaxed by playing snooker on a gyro-stabilized table – an age old joke in the Navy which none the less continues to find victims.

You could tell Andrew was in the wardroom when a film was being shown by the enormous guffaws of laughter from the 'stalls'. Not everything pleased him though. He walked out of the film *The Rose* starring Bette Midler as a drugged-up rock star muttering 'silly cow'. He neither drank nor smoked, at least in public, and while looking relaxed among his fellow pilots was perhaps inevitably conscious of his position. It is hard to feel one of the boys when your flying overalls sport the name 'HRH Prince Andrew'. He was known to his colleagues simply as 'H' and was delighted weeks later when he came ashore in Port Stanley and I referred to him as 'H'. 'I've been trying for ages to get you journalists to call me that,' he laughed. From the interviews he gave in Stanley after the fighting had finished, it almost seemed as if a different character had emerged. He was more articulate than before and less self-conscious. Perhaps the endless flying, the responsibility and the danger had matured him beyond his years.

Andrew was always amazingly smartly dressed. His clothes seemed that bit crisper than the rest of the officers', and his hair was always well cut and the same length. We wondered if there was a hairdresser on board by Royal Appointment. He had a flashing smile, *Boys Own* good looks and a physique which women's magazine writers like to describe as 'hunky'. The first day on board we were told that, 'As far as we are concerned he is like anyone else. He is just another officer.' It became apparent over a period of time that this was true. He flew dangerous missions to rescue a pilot from a ditched helicopter off *Hermes* and the survivors of the *Atlantic Conveyor* after she was hit by an Exocet. He was also apt to be called on to be 'Exocet decoy', flying his helicopter alongside *Invincible* to distract the missile and draw it away beneath the aircraft. It was a hazardous exercise that required a cool nerve, hovering twenty feet above the waves, ready to rise up above the missile's (allegedly) maximum height of twenty-seven feet as it fizzed over the horizon just below the speed of sound. On the day *Sheffield* was hit *Invincible* fired chaff from near the bridge that almost brought down the Prince's helicopter as he flew alongside. Piloting a helicopter in the South Atlantic was a dangerous operation and twenty were lost, including four Sea Kings which ditched in the ocean. But there was never any suggestion that Andrew did any more or less than the other pilots. To have treated him differently would have undermined his confidence and alienated the rest of the squadron.

On Good Friday, just four days after we sailed from Portsmouth, we heard for the first time the harsh, rasping note of the klaxon calling the ship to action stations. Men rushed down passages as if pursued by a pack of wild dogs, dragging anti-flash hoods over their heads and putting on white elbow-length gloves, like a duchess heading for a state dinner. The urgency that the klaxon conveyed was contagious and you would find yourself running, slamming down hatches as a disembodied voice kept repeating, 'Action stations, action stations. Assume NBCD state one. Condition zulu.' The initials referred to nuclear, biological and chemical defences, which meant making the ship airtight from attack. Condition zulu meant all the hatches and doors had to be sealed, a higher state of alert than 'yankee'. Sealing up *Invincible* could take anything between ten to twenty-five minutes, depending on the training of the crew. Once completed it was rather like being locked in a vast tomb, knowing escape would be hindered by sealed decks with scores of men competing to get through the 'kidney hatches'. At first we found ourselves assigned to the Damage Control Centre of the ship during action stations. This was presided over by Lt.-Com. Andy Holland, known to everyone as 'Damage', who gaily chattered about *Invincible* being able to take five Exocet hits before sinking. After some thought this seemed a bad place to be. It was right in the centre of the ship and at Exocet height. Discussing the safest position during threat of attack became an almost full-time pastime, rather in the manner that overweight people discuss the merits of diets. The press, like a lost tribe, wandered around the ship debating the chief targets, sometimes watching what was going on from the Admiral's bridge and at other times seeking refuge in the Captain's day cabin, lying on the carpets and staring at the bulkhead.

But at least we could move around in search of safety. Most of the crew had no choice but to stay in their assigned positions sweating it out. Many would try and sleep. Others would just lie there, write letters, read girlie magazines or play cards. Some were distinguishable only by their names written across the forehead of their white anti-flash hood, disguising all but their eyes. It was possible to go for days, even weeks, without tasting the salt on your lips or feeling the wind. The weather throughout continued to belie all predictions. Instead of raging seas we had fog and instead of sleet we had crisp sunny days. There were one or two gales but down in the bowels of *Invincible*, fitted with stabilizers, the roll was barely discernible. Steaming along in a large British warship had as much to do with the sea as flying has with travel in a jumbo jet. At times, it seemed, we might as well have been in a submarine. The sense of vulnerability, even claustrophobia, was impossible to avoid. Modern warships have abandoned armour plating, taking the view that the money is better spent on missile defences. One hair-raising theory that 'Damage' told us about the light construction of *Invincible*, was that an Exocet could pass right through without exploding. No one seemed keen to test the theory.

I had acquired a small cabin at the stern of the ship, just above the waterline. The escape routes from this cubicle were negligible. You had to move down a passage, through several sealed doors and then up ladders. 'It's not worth it,' one sub-lieutenant nonchalantly told me. 'All the doors will buckle if we're hit and you'll never get out.' At the outset the hacks had been placed in the Admiral's offices. This was rather like sleeping in a canning factory during an earth tremor. The rooms were full of filing cabinets and as the ship vibrated the files reverberated, as in an outlandish and off-key tintinnabulation. I tried sleeping with ear-defenders and then with cotton wool ear plugs. Neither was effective. We tried to locate the root of the noises, sticking sheets of paper between the cabinets – also with no success. Gareth Parry of the *Guardian* struggled naked over desk tops in the middle of the night, tapping the ceiling in a futile attempt to pinpoint a particularly irritating rattle. He retired to his camp bed muttering, 'Sleep is release. The nightmare starts when we wake up.'

Apart from the calls to action stations, training exercises were given greater verisimilitude with the addition of smoke canisters, thunderflashes and one pound scare charges dropped alongside the ship. 'We've got to give the men the smell of cordite,' the captain said. The mood of impending struggle was heightened with notices recommending the men to make out their wills and ensure the name of their next of kin was up-to-date on official documents. We were also issued with identity discs which gave rank, name and blood group. Later on we had to carry at all times a life jacket at our waist and a bright orange survival suit. Anti-flash hoods were worn relaxed around necks, like grubby cravats.

Many crewmen received brief courses in first aid. The ship's surgeon, Bob Clarke, gave a humorous account on television of how to shove morphine injections into your leg, ending the programme with a smile and saying 'have a good war'. Although extra supplies of plasma, morphine, antibiotics, plaster of paris and intravenous fluids were on board, Clarke said cheerfully: 'We'll decide those people who are worth saving, and make it as comfortable as possible for those who are not.' Potential hazards from whiplash, such as mirrors, glasses, and loose objects, were removed and flammable material like curtains and cushions were stowed away. *Invincible* was gradually transformed from a relatively luxurious craft, certainly far more luxurious than we had been led to expect, into an austere fighting unit, prepared for the worst.

I remember sitting in the wardroom at the end of April watching the closed-circuit television churn out a more or less continual diet of soap opera, war films, Tom and Jerry cartoons and extracts from comedy shows. Pilots, wearing their green one-piece overalls or rubber 'goon suits' to protect them against the freezing South Atlantic, lounged casually in armchairs. Some carried 9mm Browning pistols in shoulder holsters. Around them coffee tables had been piled together and tied to pillars with string. The landscape watercolours had gone from the walls and the crests above the bar removed. The cabinet case which had displayed relics of the triumphs of former HMS *Invincible*'s (including the victory off the Falklands in 1914) was now covered with brown paper on which cartoons and new trophies had been drawn, including a whale for 820 Squadron which had depth-charged one in mistake for a hostile submarine. Television programmes started with a picture of a topless girl accompanied by a Welsh male-voice choir. Someone said they used to show extracts of *Emmanuelle* before senior officers addressed the crew to ensure there was an audience.

But as we moved south to Ascension life remained good. There were drinks in the evening before dinner, a good wine list, and a four-course meal invariably followed by port. Films were shown three times a week on the screen in the dining room or wardroom. There were cocktails on the quarterdeck as the sun dipped over the horizon and sing-songs. What a way to go to war, we all thought, without actually thinking we would.

Invincible, like most large naval ships, was a self-contained world. It had its own doctors, dentists, library, television, bars, shop and entertainment. There was even a Chinese cobbler, tailor and laundry, which the fourteen Chinese on board adopted as their action station. There were hundreds of Hong Kong Chinese in the task force, mainly in the Royal Fleet Auxiliary ships. On one, *Sir Geraint*, we were served meals by a nervous Chinese steward wearing a tin helmet, his own protest at being thrust into such a war.

Different ranks would be divided into their own messes. One night with the petty officers the journalists became the butt of all the good-humoured jokes, staggering out without our ties which joined an already impressive array of trophies. Even though they were rationed to three cans of beer a day, they would not allow us to buy a drink. Whenever a glass of lager appeared someone would produce a small bottle and pour a wicked substance into it with a huge grin. They cursed the officers as incompetent, the ship as badly designed and their fate as grim. None of them really wanted to fight but if they had to they would.

At the Equator we were summoned to meet King Neptune and his court, who arrived on the flight deck on the huge hydraulic lift used for the Harriers and Sea Kings. Several were sentenced to have a foul substance smeared on their faces and dumped backwards into a canvas swimming pool. Among the victims were the Captain, Prince Andrew, the pressmen and their 'minder', the Ministry of Defence press officer who had taken to the bridge in the futile hope of escaping the 'policemen' who roamed the ship.

On 16 April Ascension emerged from the Atlantic, a barren volcanic rock basking in the tropical sun. Instead of the task force fleet anchored offshore as we had expected, there were only a few ships, including HMS *Fearless*, the home of Commodore Michael Clapp and the future base of Maj.-Gen. Jeremy Moore. The rest of the fleet, it later emerged, had moved on at speed when it appeared that a diplomatic settlement was likely. The government wanted to get as many ships as far south as possible in case an agreement ruled they could move no closer to the Falklands. There was certainly a sense of urgency. Before we had anchored, helicopters were ferrying out supplies, slung beneath the aircraft like huge shopping bags. In the distance Hercules could be seen taking off and landing at Wideawake airfield. Crewmen took the opportunity to drop a line over the stern and sat up all night, catching vicious fish, including a shark which broke a rod in three places. The only excitement came when two chefs from a supply ship who were taking the air spotted what they thought was a periscope and for a couple of hours threw the fleet into pandemonium. *Hermes* and other ships went to action stations as frigates and helicopters pursued a solid sonar contact travelling at fifteen knots. 'At that speed it's got to be nuclear-powered,' one officer said authoritatively. We all wondered if we had found a Russian submarine sneaking in for a close-up. Their Tupolev aircraft, after all, had for some time been brazenly buzzing the fleet taking photographs. But after some heavy 'pinging' with sonar it was decided the underwater object was a whale and the two chefs had been hallucinating. Whales, in fact, got a pretty hard time all the way down. They were always being mistaken for submarines and being depth-charged and torpedoed. It became so common to detect them that one of the first and few jokes of the war was 'It's all over lads. The whales have surrendered.'

Instead of spending several days at Ascension, as planned, *Invincible* suddenly upped anchor and set off south on 18 April. Captain J.J. Black had said there was no Rubicon in the operation, but it suddenly seemed we had passed the point of no return and war appeared likely. The Captain was a master of the colourful, pithy phrase. Although at the outset he said 'we'll piss it' he was undoubtedly concerned and had pinpointed the Super Etendards carrying Exocets as a major threat. A large, slightly balding man with sharp blue eyes, he had an American-style baseball cap with J.J. Black emblazoned across the back, which he sometimes wore on top of his white anti-flash hood, and drank tea from a mug with

'Boss' on the side. He was a highly thoughtful seaman who had seen service in Korea, Malaya and Borneo and had drawn up the rules of engagement for war. Apart from speaking good German and French, he was teaching himself Spanish. Like many military men he saw the value of the press to help the war effort but was not happy if that press freedom strayed into sensitive areas. On one occasion he described us as one of his weapons systems in the fight against Argentina.

The Captain said that *Brilliant, Glasgow, Sheffield* and *Coventry* had been waiting for us at Ascension but had moved south at speed 'to stake out a line' in case of a diplomatic settlement. We then sailed with *Hermes*, which Admiral Sandy Woodward had joined from *Glamorgan, Broadsword, Alacrity* and several supply vessels. The task force was moving south towards the Falklands to establish air and sea superiority before the amphibious forces followed, lessening the risk to unprotected troops.

Many crewmen were surprised to find the journalists still on board after Ascension. Apart from the general assumption that we would abandon ship before things became dangerous, the most common question, always delivered with a note of incredulity, was if we had volunteered for the operation or had been 'press-ganged'. When we replied we had not declined the offer, they treated us either as deranged madmen or warmongers. The next question would be along the lines of 'I suppose you blokes are being paid a fucking fortune to be out here?' To deny it merely provoked disbelief.

Soon after leaving Ascension we had our first encounter with Argentina. A Boeing 707 in military colours located the fleet before being intercepted by an armed Harrier. The early surveillance came as a surprise to the task force so far north and it was only the government warning that 'appropriate action' would be taken that stopped them after a few days. The tempo was now quickening and it seemed the government was ready for a full-scale attack if diplomatic talks failed. For some time the Captain had said there was concern about the task force having their hands tied but we saw no sign of this; only of resolution from the government or, perhaps more accurately, Mrs Thatcher.

The fleet transferred to battle formation as we moved through the

Roaring Forties, with three frigates and destroyers forming the spearhead or 'picket'. In the centre of a defensive screen the two carriers, dogged by their 'goalkeepers', *Brilliant* and *Broadsword*, sat like queen bees. On 25 April we picked up the first news of the retaking of South Georgia and learnt that the SAS and the SBS had landed on the island days earlier but had lost two helicopters in a blizzard. It was here that the SAS had called for extra hand-grenades and a box was flown in. When the soldier opened it he found tea cups.

The SAS operation on South Georgia very nearly came unstuck. They had joined the task force at Ascension, D Squadron boarding the supply ship *Fort Austin*. They were followed by G Squadron, officered and manned almost entirely by members of the Household Division. In all 126 men were sent. The SAS headquarters stayed at the planning centre of the operation aboard HMS *Fearless*, even though until the landing several thousand miles separated the ship from the rest of the unit.

On 18 April, fifteen men left a warship in five Gemini rubber boats to land on Grass Island within sight of one of the Argentine bases on South Georgia. The Geminis were powered by Johnson 40 outboard motors. They were considered notoriously unreliable and the SAS had complained about them for years. Three of the engines broke down on the journey ashore. One of the Geminis was swept away into the darkness by gale force winds and the three-man crew spent the night adrift before being rescued the following day by helicopter. The second Gemini crew managed to drag themselves on to the last piece of South Georgia before Antarctica and lay low for five days until they were sure the island was taken before they radioed for help. The third boat was towed ashore by the others and the nine men lay up signalling reports to the fleet. The intelligence the SAS provided persuaded them to go for a surprise attack on the Argentinian positions.

The special services were to continue to play a vital role in the war. On 1 May, the first SAS and SBS patrols went on to the Falklands to test the lie of the land in advance of the task force assault. 'Getting on the islands was a real psychological barrier,' one of them recalled later. 'No one knew how good they were or whether there wouldn't be a reception party to scarf you up when you arrived. It was like being the first people on the moon. You didn't know whether you were going to disappear into thirty feet of dust or find some hard standing.'

Three patrols concentrated on Port Stanley. The remainder reconnoitred around Port Howard, Fox Bay, Goose Green and Bluff Cove. They hid during the day and at night moved in close to study the Argentinian defences coming within a hundred yards of their troops.

Back on the ships, the daily intelligence briefs grew fatter as the SAS reports filtered back. Some of them were remarkably accurate, especially the picture they built up of the Argentine garrison at Stanley. Troop positions, artillery and armour were all exactly described. But there were also morale-boosting reports of dysentery, food shortages and near mutiny among the conscripts that were subsequently shown to be wide of the mark.

For the SAS, the Falklands war was a return to the role that they were originally designed for by their inventor Colonel David Stirling in the Second World War – long-range operations behind enemy lines, and a diversion from the anti-terrorist operations and training of Third World armies that had preoccupied them for the preceding decade. At Pebble Island they showed they were still masters at it. The island had been identified by naval radar and Harriers as the main diversionary airfield for Argentine planes flying to Port Stanley from the mainland. Rear Admiral Woodward's enthusiasm for the raid was only lukewarm at first, as he was preoccupied with the battle in the air. The first operation to put a patrol on the island was stood down shortly before the helicopter carrying the men was due to take off.

The six-man patrol that landed on West Falkland on 7 May had to make a slow approach to avoid detection. The SAS commander was on the point of aborting the mission as the men were needed for pre-landing recces on East Falkland. Then at four o'clock on the afternoon of 12 May the patrol radioed through to say they had found the Argentinians. That night the rest of D Squadron was flown in. They marched for two hours across the island while a warship pummelled the defenders' positions with shellfire. When they left, eleven planes had been destroyed and two SAS men wounded – apart from Captain John Hamilton, the unit's only combat casualties of the war. Hamilton was killed charging an Argentine machine gun post on West Falkland just before the ceasefire. The SAS also lost nineteen men from G Squadron when a helicopter crashed into the sea the day before the landings.

By the end of the campaign the SAS had reverted to their contemporary role. The preliminaries to the fall of Stanley were conducted by them very much as if the task force were the police and the Argentinians a desperate terrorist band holed up with a large number of hostages.

On Friday, 30 April, we were told the task force would launch attacks the next day on the Falklands and that three frigates would start a naval bombardment. The carriers would stay in the north-eastern corner of the 200 mile zone, the farthest point for land-based Argentine aircraft to reach. 'I'm sure we'll hit them very much harder than they've expected and we'll soon have them back at the negotiating table keen for a diplomatic solution,' Commander Tony Provest, the second-in-command, said.

For us, the war started the next morning, at 7.44 a.m. gmt, about three hours before dawn. (Throughout the voyage the task force had used 'zulu time' or gmt, and as a result we were getting up at about 3 a.m. local time and going to bed at about 9 p.m. local.) A Vulcan bomber, codenamed 'Black Buck' and flying all the way from Ascension Island refuelled by Victor tankers, dropped twenty-one 1,000 pound bombs on Stanley airfield. Only one hit the runway and the raids were repeated later in the war, with no more success. From the bridge you could see the Harriers being prepared for battle, the yellow tip on the Sidewinder missiles beneath the wings showing they were armed. At 8.15 the flight controller told a helicopter pilot: 'The Vulcan has gone in. We are now at war.' At that moment the departure from Portsmouth more than three weeks earlier belonged to another existence. At 9.05 four Harriers took off, their jets burning brightly against the clear, starry sky. They were to fly CAP (combat air patrol) while the Harriers from *Hermes*, who were expecting to lose three planes, would hit Port Stanley airfield with high explosives and cluster bombs. Others would attack Goose Green, thought to be the main base for the Pucara, the dangerous counter-insurgency aircraft.

The pilots from the first excursion looked tense although they had seen no enemy planes. The dawn came up slowly, its pink fingers curling over the horizon revealing a calm sea. Soon afterwards we had our first air raid warning and were told that Argentine Mirages had been 'splashed'. The announcements throughout that long and tense day tended to paint a rather more serious picture of events, with reports of Super Etendards unleashing Exocets at incredible ranges of 140 miles. (This later turned out to be missiles fired at one of the Harriers.) On the bridge we wore our anti-flash and scanned the horizon for enemy planes, chewing toffees. An officer held up a picture of a Mirage so we would know what they looked like. There were continual games of cat and mouse over the horizon as the Argentine jets tested the fleet's responses, veering away when they were intercepted by Harriers. We were frequently warned: 'There is a possible air raid building in the west. On anti-flash.' After long minutes we were told, 'It's all right. The Harriers have chased them away.' In the meantime the bombardment of Stanley airfield continued. Crewmen broke off for 'action snacks', drank their tea from 'action mugs' and then headed for 'action messing'. The word had become something of a joke and they now looked forward to an 'action smoke' with their 'action pint'.

It was a day of confusion. At 5.45 p.m. with a weak winter sun washing over the ship, we were told our Harriers had attacked a submarine close to the Falklands. Moments later we were informed it was a rock formation which looked like a submarine.

It was also a day of some success. It had shown the Argentinians what the task force was capable of and only one Harrier from *Hermes* got a bullet through its tail. The rest returned undamaged. In the evening Paul Barton, an RAF pilot attached to 801 Squadron, shot down a Mirage with a Sidewinder missile and a Canberra with three men on board was also splashed by Alan Curtis, who a few days later died in an air collision. The Argentinians said they had destroyed eleven Harriers, two helicopters and had damaged several ships and an aircraft carrier. In fact only two ships were slightly damaged by bombs and cannons. A Lynx helicopter, which was directing naval guns, was also hit by machine gun fire. The main task force came under attack from three Canberras which were driven off, one shot down and another limping home.

The next morning we went to precautionary action stations

because the Argentinian fleet was thought to be steaming towards us for a full confrontation. For most of the war the Argentine carrier *25th of May* had been shadowed by one of the nuclear-powered submarines but it had apparently managed to slip their cover. It was thought to be 220 miles to the north-west and was expected to launch a low level dawn strike with eight aircraft. The padre, Bill Wheldon, known as 'Bill the Bish', came over the tannoy just before dawn to say a prayer. It was meant to raise morale on what was said to be a 'very testing day', in fact it was so mournful that a sense of dread hung over the carrier. With no sign of the enemy the tension changed to anti-climax.

That evening a film in the wardroom was interrupted by a cheer from a group of helicopter pilots, punching their fists in the air like soccer supporters. 'They'll be doing the widow's hop in Buenos Aires tonight,' one pilot shouted. News had come through that the Argentine cruiser, *General Belgrano*, had been torpedoed by HMS *Conqueror*. That initial euphoria, however, soon changed to shock when the BBC reported that most of the crew of 1,000 men could have perished. It seemed an incredible loss of life, and although the figure was later revised to 300, the war was now all too vicious. 'We are all sailors. We all wear our life jackets and we know what it would be like,' Lieutenant Richard Aylard, the Captain's secretary, said. 'It is something we would not wish on anybody.' At the same time a Lynx helicopter using the new Sea Skua missile sank an Argentine patrol boat which had fired on a Sea King. The Argentinians had been offered the Skua before the crisis, but had declined it saying they wanted more proof that it was effective.

Britain's string of successes, however, was about to receive a serious setback. On Tuesday, 3 May, we were called to action stations at 2.15 p.m. with the news that there were air raids from the south-west with two planes at sixty miles and closing. After a long pause an excited voice came over the tannoy and said bluntly: 'The *Sheffield* may have been hit.' At 2.22 he again reported there was a possibility of an air strike. *Invincible* was vibrating heavily, weaving through the water as she picked up speed and turned to face the threat.

Brilliant, our goalkeeper, her Sea Wolf missiles twitching, was a few hundred yards astern. At 2.31 we were told: '*Sheffield* has been hit by an air-launched Exocet. They are fighting the fire and she is about fifteen to twenty miles to the south-west of us. We are transferring fire-fighting equipment from *Invincible*.'

Suddenly we saw the frigate *Yarmouth* firing chaff, metallic strips designed to confuse the radar-guidance system on a missile, and watched the canisters tumbling into the sea. For a moment it looked as if she was under attack and rockets were splashing around her. We hit the deck, not knowing what was happening, lying on our backs and thinking how exposed we were on the bridge and how thin the hull was. There were tremendous 'whooshes' and we thought missiles were flying past. 'We are under missile attack. I say again we are under missile attack,' the voice said over the tannoy. We prayed silently. One seaman, lying alongside us in a narrow passageway, said: 'Never mind mate. If it hits, it hits. You won't know anything about it.' At last the tannoy announced: 'The picture is somewhat confused but there are no missiles in flight. There are no missiles in flight.' Having braced ourselves for the explosion we waited, and only slowly did the tension ease from our bodies. I looked at my notebook and saw that all I had written for long minutes was 'WHOOSH' in big letters, and 'terrifying'. A colleague had just noted, with admirable self-restraint, 'periods of intense anxiety'.

From the bridge we could see ships zig-zagging to evade torpedo attack and on the horizon a pall of smoke from the *Sheffield* rose to the clouds. *Glasgow* had 'seen' a submarine periscope and was busy depth-charging the area. Harriers took off to intercept further contacts and Sea Kings were ferrying men off *Sheffield* and trying to fight the fire raging through the ship. We wondered how elated the pilot of the Super Etendard must have felt (in fact he did not immediately know he had hit a ship) and tried not to think what was happening on *Sheffield*. It was a bad time. When someone slammed a door we jumped.

There were further alerts throughout that afternoon but no threat materialized. Two missiles had been fired and the planes had immediately turned for home. *Sheffield* had no more than four seconds' warning but ships close to her had time to fire chaff, which had possibly deflected the other Exocet to crash harmlessly into the sea. As the afternoon wore on, fear gave way to rather black humour. We thought of putting a message from *The Times* on a Sidewinder missile. The *Sun* had already sponsored one saying 'Up yours, Galtieri'. We decided the imaginary *Times* Sidewinder would say: 'You are a despicable cad, General'. Someone wanted to rename the ship HMS *Humble* because he thought HMS *Invincible* was provocative; 'It explains why the four previous ones were sunk,' he said.

Later the order came for *Sheffield* to be abandoned because of the danger of her Sea Dart missiles exploding. The survivors, and there were many more than people expected, gathered on the deck singing, 'You've got to look on the bright side of life.' At first we feared that perhaps eighty had died in the explosion but the figure was quickly reduced to twenty. Crewmen said if she had been at action stations more would have perished including the Captain, Sam Salt. He later said he only had enough time to shout 'take cover'. Within twenty seconds the ship was full of black, acrid smoke from burning cables, paint and the missile's unused jet fuel. Although they tried to save *Sheffield* to research the effects of missile damage she sank in heavy seas as she was being towed by a tug, the water washing in through the gaping hole in her starboard side. Lessons were already being applied to other ships of the task force. We had to start carrying our gas masks to help us escape through smoke, and the air pressure in the ship was increased. Each of the three citadels was sealed off and it was hoped the pressure would drive smoke back out of the hole made by a missile.

The attack on the *Sheffield* profoundly shocked the Navy. They knew Argentina had air-launched Exocets but thought they lacked the capability to use them effectively, largely because they had just been delivered by their manufacturers in France. The Captain said they could only carry out two more such attacks but the Argentinian Air Force was to launch several more Exocet raids, sinking *Atlantic Conveyor*. It also brought home the vulnerability of the ships. If the planes evaded our radar, which due to absence of an airborne early warning system, was not too difficult, they could only be taken out by Sea Dart missiles or guns. Neither was very effective and the most advanced defence, the Sea Wolf missile, was only fitted on two ships. As a result warships had to resort to such touch-and-go systems as chaff, the Exocet decoy and turning head-on to the threat to minimize damage. It was decided that the Exocet's guidance system could be confused by two radar blips alongside each other and as a missile scanned from side to side seeking a target it could be tempted towards the Exocet decoy or helicopter. Whether the system worked is another matter.

Apart from this new and deadly air threat, the task force was also in constant danger of submarine attack. One Argentinian submarine was destroyed at South Georgia but they had three others, and at least one was suspected of being off the Falklands.

On 5 May we went to precautionary action stations before dawn. At 11.55 we were told: 'On anti-flash. There is a possible torpedo, possible torpedo.' The *Invincible* speeded up to thirty knots, shuddering with the strain to her 19,500 ton bulk, and began weaving back and forth. 'We are avoiding torpedoes,' a cryptic announcement said. We looked astern but could see nothing. Commander Provest came on the tannoy, his voice measured as ever, 'HMS *Brilliant* detected or thought she detected a submarine to the south. Our speed is now such that we would outrun any torpedo. There is therefore no imminent danger.' The idea of the carrier being faster than a torpedo conjured up absurd images of a Morris Minor of a weapon, trundling along hopelessly after us through the South Atlantic. It later emerged that for most of the conflict the three Argentine submarines were in port undergoing repair, or close to the mainland. The task force spent thousands of man hours and huge quantities of fuel pursuing phantoms beneath the waves.

For the next few days the fleet was enveloped in thick mist yet continued to fly Harriers in conditions that would have been shunned in peacetime. It was during one of these fogs that two Harriers apparently collided. Lt.-Com. John Eyton-Jones, known to everyone as EJ, and Lieutenant Alan Curtis were flying CAP twenty-five miles apart, when a helicopter at sea level noted an air contact passing and told the two Harriers, who went down to investigate. Nothing more was heard and no wreckage was found. That night the Harrier pilots gathered in the bar, a tight-knit group laughing and joking among themselves. 'It's the only way we can keep going and not go completely crazy,' was how one of them described it later. EJ was an amusing, extrovert character, with boyish looks and a sharp wit. He was the warfare instructor, an experienced pilot who had given us a 'film show' on how the Harriers took on F15s and beat them in mock combat. Al Curtis was more shy, a thoroughly nice man who was genuinely upset when he shot down a Canberra bomber. His wife was pregnant and two months later photographs of her appeared in the newspapers with her new-born child. For people who knew both men, it was one of the most heart-wrenching moments of the war. A memorial service was held in the hangar among the paraphernalia of war, with a Harrier sitting at the end.

There was a discernible change among Harrier pilots as they flew endless sorties to check out radar contacts and bomb land targets. The commanding officer of 801 Squadron was Nigel 'Sharky' Ward, a bearded, slight man with a shark-like grin and an irrepressible sense of confidence and leadership. If he had not been a pilot he would have been salesman of the year. Sharky was the master of the provocative quote, lying in his bunk dreaming up sayings. Other pilots, asked for comments from journalists, would go to him for inspiration. He once came up to me with a grin, 'I've got another good one for you. The Argentinians,' he said slowly, so I could remember it, 'are like splash targets in the sky. Go tell 'em that.' The quotes were so good that the Ministry of Defence sent telegrams to congratulate him. 'You've got to be a bit of a cowboy to be a pilot,' he explained. 'We call the helicopter pilots "farmers". Fighter pilots have to be able to peel a banana with their left hand while juggling with their right.' He relished the idea of a small war. It was quite a sight to see him slide out of his cockpit, walk across the pitching deck of the carrier with a grin on his face. Like other squadron leaders he was called 'Boss' and loved it. He celebrated his thirty-eighth birthday on the voyage and his elevation to the rank of commander. Some of his quotes were grossly over-optimistic, such as 'air superiority should be easy to achieve'. But he was no fool and was simply playing the propaganda game.

The Harrier pilots were distinguishable in some indefinable way from other crewmen. Many had had mixed careers. Ian Mortimer, for instance, an RAF pilot attached to the Fleet Air Arm, was the most experienced with 1,200 hours in a Harrier before we sailed. He had been in his own words a 'bum' after getting a degree in physics

51

and had decided to join the RAF on the spur of the moment. Mike Watson, looking like a thirties screen lover with his hair slicked back, had come through the ranks and made his first landing on a carrier soon after we left Portsmouth. Charlie Cantan, the baby of the squadron at twenty-seven, was known as 'Champagne Charlie' and seen as a man with friends in high places.

For the pilots it was the nearest thing to single combat since the Battle of Britain, except that here the odds were worse. On the way down they became more introspective, drank less and smoked more. One of them would anxiously ask us if there was going to be a diplomatic settlement. Although at that stage it seemed unlikely, we told him there was a good chance and he seemed relieved. You had only to stand above the flight deck and watch them sitting in their cramped cockpits throughout the night staring at the sky, waiting to be scrambled and meet a fate that depended on the speed of their reactions pinpointing a flickering enemy swinging before their sights to realize the pressures. By the time of the ceasefire *Invincible* had lost four Harriers, three in accidents including one which crashed on take-off with a lucky escape for the pilot. Mortimer's was shot down by ground fire near Stanley. He ejected and was rescued from the sea. They had also shot down several planes. Ward claimed three kills; a Mirage, Pucara and Hercules, whose crew he was said to have waved to before he shot it down.

There were constant reminders, though, that air superiority was elusive and threats of Argentine air raids continued. A typical one, which would rarely lead to an attack, would be along the lines of, 'Enemy aircraft have been spotted sixty miles to the west. They do not appear to have closed with us. There are further contacts to the west at about 100 miles. The air raid warning remains red.' The Captain freely admitted the air battle was going to be long and difficult, mainly because the Argentinians had more planes and were not being drawn into combat with the Harriers, who had shown themselves to be far more manoeuvrable. 'We will just have to whittle away at it,' he said.

We had also strayed across Argentina's rather amateur attempt at spying on the fleet using a requisitioned trawler called *Narwhal*. This had been taken over by their Navy to send back coded reports about our position. The code was simple but effective. An aircraft carrier was a 'sardine', a plane a 'salmon', a helicopter a 'herring' and so on. The *Narwhal*, however, had strayed into the 200 mile zone around the islands and was cannoned and bombed by Harriers from *Hermes*. Most of the men were simple fishermen and terrified by the experience, although they also obviously had a sense of humour because on board a picture of Mrs Thatcher had been turned into a dartboard. One was killed in the attack and the rest were brought back by the SBS to the *Invincible* where the dead man was buried at sea. The early morning service was translated into Spanish by Sub-Lieutenant Matthew Taylor, the son of the British ambassador to Bonn, Sir Jock Taylor. Many of the fishermen broke down and cried, hugging each other as the body, wrapped in a canvas bag and draped with the Argentinian flag, slid over the side and floated into the damp mist shrouding the ship. The men, their shoelaces removed and blankets around their shoulders, shouted '*Viva la Patria, viva Argentina*', before trooping back for confinement in the chapel. Most refused to believe they were on *Invincible*, having been told several times that it had been sunk.

As the task force sought to tighten its blockade it sent ships farther west. During a sortie down the Falkland Sound between the two islands a frigate sank what appeared to be a fuel or ammunition ship sailing with no lights. There was a large explosion and no sign of survivors. On 12 May, *Glasgow* and *Brilliant* were on the gun line off Stanley lobbing in a few shells when they came under attack from four Skyhawks. Two were shot down by Sea Wolf missiles and the third apparently got such a surprise it spun away and crashed into the sea. It was claimed the fourth plane was shot down by the Argentinians by mistake. A second wave of bombers came in and the Sea Wolf this time failed to work. *Glasgow* had an unexploded bomb pass through her stern and had to limp back nursing a three-foot hole and plugging the gap with mattresses. Once again the Skyhawks came in but by this time the fleet had scrambled its Harriers and the planes avoided combat.

The fleet, meanwhile, was gathering for what Admiral Sandy Woodward had called the 'heavy punch'. At that time a largish fleet of about nine ships was on the outer edge of the 200 mile zone waiting for the main armada to join them, including *Fearless, Intrepid, Canberra* and *Atlantic Conveyor*, carrying the vital extra

Harriers, helicopters and supplies for the landing. Other ships were still leaving Ascension and a further eleven had sailed from Britain on 10 May. The task force was now bracing itself for an Argentine counter-offensive. 'To date the Argies have very much reacted to what we have done,' Tony Provest said. 'They may decide to weaken us while they can before any more reinforcements come down.' No attacks came, however, and the Argentinians bided their time, waiting for the landing. Sandy Woodward intended to keep up the pressure a week before the landings and then the force would move north to the edge of the 200 mile zone where we would rendezvous, 'sanitize' the area of any submarines and make the final plans – the biggest naval grouping since Suez.

Provest said they had intercepted messages showing arguments between General Mario Menendez, the military governor, and air force commanders on the mainland over the lack of air cover: 'The commanders on the islands have been feeling very lonely and crying for help.' When the landing took place the invasion force would move west to San Carlos, while the carrier group travelled south-west overnight to make the Argentinians think the landing was coming south of Port Stanley.

On Thursday, 20 May, we were listening to the BBC World Service talking about eleventh-hour diplomatic moves to reach a settlement when Provest came over the tannoy to make an announcement. In a deadpan voice he said: 'The cabinet has been meeting this morning and we have just had a signal to say the landing will occur at 6.30 a.m. tomorrow morning.'

2

Sailing

After all the pomp of the fleet's departure, the *Canberra*'s send-off had an endearing amateurish quality to it. She scarcely looked very martial lying hugely along Southampton Dock with pallets groaning with Scotch swaying into her holds. We set sail five days behind the Navy on a drizzly Good Friday. About 250 wives, parents and girlfriends gathered on the quayside, not a huge crowd but enough to touch the departing troops. The lights of the television cameras cut through the gloom, lingering on the chests of two buxom girls wearing T-shirts printed with the message: 'Give the Argies some Bargy.'

A Royal Marine and a Para band took it in turns to play appropriate tunes: 'Land of Hope and Glory', 'A Life on the Ocean Wave' and the Paras' battle hymn, 'The Ride of the Valkyries'.

At 8 p.m. *Canberra* slipped anchor and moved slowly out into Southampton Water. The mournful strains of the band and the sound of cheering floating after us was gradually drowned out by the kitchen boys, yelling football chants in the bows.

Six days before, the *Canberra* had been propelling 2,000 elderly sun-seekers through the Mediterranean. The requisition order had come through while she was at Gibraltar and she put about directly for Southampton where Vosper Thornycroft workers welded a helicopter pad on to the sun deck, laid the foundations for another forward of the bridge and fitted her with valves so she could take on fuel from the Royal Fleet Auxiliary oiler that hovered about us like a pilot fish all the way to Ascension.

Strangely, nothing was ever done about *Canberra*'s colour. Her enormous white bulk and yellow twin funnels stuck out among the grey hulls of the fleet like the bull's-eye at the centre of a target. Even after twelve weeks at war the military was never quite able to iron out all the regrettable softness in the ship's character and when she sailed back into Southampton, rust-stained and with her decks scarred and broken, she remained determinedly civilian.

The first night was full of gaiety and suppressed excitement. Drink flowed freely in the ship's bars. In the senior NCOs' mess, a Marine sergeant declared: 'This is the best thing that's ever happened to me. I've been in twenty years and I'd given up hope that I'd ever see a shot fired in anger in a proper war.'

Upstairs in the Crowsnest, the *Canberra*'s poshest bar, the officers were saying much the same. War meant promotions, medals and the chance to do what they were paid for.

There were 2,800 men on board made up of 40 and 42 Commando of the Royal Marines, the Third Battalion of the Parachute Regiment and accompanying batteries from the Royal Artillery. The juxtaposition was thought unfortunate by some, given the tradition of rivalry between the Paras and the Marines. There were worries among the senior officers that if the ship turned about without a shot being fired the men might fight each other. Apart from good-natured bitching in the ship's bars about each other's incompetence, glory-seeking and stupidity there was little sign of friction on the voyage out. Hostility did not emerge until after the war was over. After Port Stanley fell there were many bitter accusations flying between the two units; the Paras claiming the Marines had a soft war, the Marines accusing the Paras of recklessness during the attack on Mount Longdon and throwing away soldiers' lives. The feeling was real enough for the two forces to be separated on the way home, with the Marines returning on *Canberra* and the Paras on *Norland*.

The night before the *Canberra* sailed the journalists held a sweepstake on the date when the ship would turn to come home. My bet was it would be within a week. The longest was 27 May. Every day at sea brought a new and unwelcome reminder that the prospect of a fight was getting less and less remote. Two days out from Southampton we picked up a Russian spy ship, the Advanced Information Gathering vessel *Evgenia* which trailed behind us, just over the horizon, for the next 4,000 miles. Her appearance surprised none of the naval officers on board, but to the rest of us it was another proof that the exercise was in earnest.

The days took on their own noisy rhythm. As dawn broke the ship started to throb with the noise of Marines and Paras running in step around and around the deck. There were permanent PT sessions and in every room and corner NCOs were putting men through weapons drills or delivering blood-curdling lectures. 'What do you do if you find a wounded Argie?' asked a Para corporal, rhetorically, to a platoon tactics talk. 'You blow his fucking head off. What do you do if there's a TV crew watching? You treat him as one of your own.' It was, I was assured, a joke.

In the evening each group on board retreated to its territorial watering hole, the men to the William Fawcett room to drink their ration of three tins of beer, the sergeants to the bar in the Meridian Room, the officers to the Crowsnest. The journalists, being honorary captains, used the Crowsnest. There were fifteen of us in all. At first we were regarded with mild suspicion and hostility by some of the officers, particularly those of us from the 'pinko press'. Their natural, keen curiosity, though, quickly broke this down. They were as fascinated with us as we were with them. To consolidate the rapprochement, the journalists gave a champagne party for each of the units, that was solemnly reciprocated later in the voyage. Most of the press corps were less than forty years old and belonged to a generation that had had less to do with the military than any other in British history. The officers came as a surprise. I had vaguely imagined a group of gently-bred, ill-educated reactionaries. It was true that some of them spoke in that contorted way that made the order 'fan out' sound like 'fair night', that the troops could mimic so well, but among the Marine officers in particular there were many who spoke in the same accents as their men. Many had been to university and had joined up not as a *faut de mieux* but because they could not stand the tedium of civilian life. They were Tories to a man, but in an *Economist*-reading sort of way. The further up the hierarchy you went, though, the more the natural order of the British military asserted itself. All the commanding officers were public school educated; Hew Pike, for instance, commanding officer of 3 Para, went to Winchester, and Colonel H. Jones was an Old Etonian. The military force commander on *Canberra*, Colonel Seccombe, was a sleek and amusing figure, steeped in the novels of Evelyn Waugh. He could quote at length from them at appropriate moments. The presence of the hacks gave him plenty of opportunity to recite passages from *Scoop*. Our sensitive egos and importunate demands put him in mind of the French film crew in Ishmaelia: 'We must protest. We have protested. Then we must protest again! We must demonstrate!' His naval opposite number was Captain Christopher Burne, known to all as Fawlty. He looked like the headmaster of a school dispensing a particularly muscular brand of Christianity and despite the fact that he was getting to the end of his career and had been recalled from a desk job at the Admiralty, he approached his command with relentless enthusiasm. There was a popular story that on his first command he ordered a rating to leap over the rail so that the ship could test her 'man overboard' drill. The man sensibly refused, whereupon Captain Burne leaped into the sea himself.

After a slow start the military suddenly grasped the publicity potential of the episode. Here was a golden opportunity to deal a painful blow against an older enemy than the Argentinians: the defence cuts. Everyone had a story of their ravages. The Marine band which played most nights somewhere around the ship was due to be broken up when the *Canberra* returned because it was a luxury that could no longer be afforded. 45 Commando who were due to go on an Arctic warfare training exercise earlier in the year that would have been perfect preparation for the Falklands had been baulked because there was not enough cash.

Each unit appointed a Public Relations Officer. The pressmen found themselves being badgered by PR men in uniform offering 'stories'. Special training sessions and presentations were laid on for the cameras. The Paras and Marines vied with each other for the hacks' favours.

Of all the troops the senior officers were the most cautious and the least bellicose. The common view among them was that the best solution would be a diplomatic settlement because it would prove the deterrent effect of strong armed forces. There was some doubt about the wisdom of the enterprise. 'It is one thing to die for Queen and country and another to die for Margaret Thatcher,' said a senior officer one evening.

In general, people were looking forward to the chance of firing at real humans and blasting real tanks, though this was rarely stated. No one bothered to disguise their worries about how horrible it might turn out to be. One night we were talking about torture: 'They would only have to show me the electrodes and I would be screaming for a shorthand taker,' said a Para Lieutenant, who bore a strong resemblance to the young Lord Kitchener. I next heard of him being shot through the thigh on Mount Longdon while he was standing in open ground urging his men forward to another attack on an Argentine position.

The small detachment of Blues and Royals on board conformed most closely to their popular image. There were two lieutenants, Lord Robin Innes-Kerr and Mark Coreth, filling in a few years in the Guards before farming or going into the City. They talked about the tank crews as their 'boys'. Their concern about whether they were getting properly fed and watered made them sound as if they were a string of hunters.

The men spoke with the accents of Britain's unemployment black-spots, particularly Glasgow and Tyneside. There were surprisingly few Londoners or blacks. The officers freely admitted that black recruits were subjected to continual insults by the NCOs and the rest of the men, but a blind eye was turned to it on the grounds that: 'If they can't hack that they won't make Marines.' Even after the training was over black soldiers had to put up with almost perpetual casual abuse of the sort that English people always defend as friendly banter but which would provoke violence if directed at them. On top of Mount Challenger I saw a black marine whose head was frosted with droplets of mist. 'You look like a bottle of Guinness,' someone said.

Many of the Toms, as the Para officers called their men with a mixture of affection and contempt, enjoyed their image as emotionless, efficient killers, one step away from being psychopaths. They wore skinhead haircuts and when out of uniform, carefully tattered sweatshirts. The Para words for this look were 'ruggsy' or 'warry'. The style owed a lot to the Vietnam war. When the sun shone and they were running round the deck, some of the Toms would wind cloth bands round their foreheads to stop the sweat dripping into their eyes, just like Robert de Niro in *The Deerhunter*. This turned out to be one of the troops' favourite films and played to packed audiences in the ship's cinema.

There were scores of films on board and every single one of them involved massive destruction and carnage. Every night somewhere around the ship, World War II was being replayed on celluloid. The officers and men made rather childish audiences, yelling and whooping when the baddies got blown away. I asked one Para, a heavily tattooed private from Bournemouth called Barry who had joined the regiment after abandoning an apprenticeship as a fitter and a flirtation with the French Foreign Legion, what he would do if he found a wounded Argie. 'Kill him with me bayonet, rip his gold teeth out and cut his fingers off to get his rings,' he replied. Of course they did nothing of the sort when the hypothesis became real. But they would like you to think they would.

The Paras reckoned they could sustain fifty per cent casualties without morale being fatally affected. 3 Para proved the calculation was correct, but only just. They kept fighting hard after Mount Longdon, where the battalion lost twenty-two men, but long after the shooting was over they talked obsessively and darkly about the experience.

One of the most impressive members of 3 Para was Corporal Jeremy Phillips, their star sniper. Corporal Phillips had a brown muscular face, a powerful simian body and a great enthusiasm for his work. He had spent time patrolling IRA bandit country in South Armagh and could put ten bullets in a target an inch across at 100 metres. He explained in a quiet voice that the snipers' purpose was not solely to kill the enemy but to do it in a manner that would dispirit them. It was best to aim at the man with the map and the binoculars, because the chances were he would be an officer. 'Shooting at the latrines while the enemy is defecating is a good time, sir,' he explained, 'because that's when they least expect it. After a time they become too frightened to go to the toilet and start defecating around the trenches which leads to disease and such like.' Corporal Phillips was hit in the shoulder by Argentinian shellfire on Mount Longdon.

It seemed it was a reflex for the men to accept their officer's discipline, although the Toms had a reputation for being more difficult than the 'Booties' as the Marines were called, and occasionally there were stories of startling rebellions with three or four men ganging up on unpopular officers (though none happened during the war). Some of the men talked about 'fragging' officers they disliked during a firefight. The most popular candidate was an officer who had risen from the ranks

The Para officers treated their men well, but with a paternalism that bordered on contempt. 'They have to have everything done for them,' was a frequent complaint. 'If there's something wrong with the chips in the mess they come and tell us.'

The certainties of institutional life were the main attractions for some of the men. Sitting in a slit trench in San Carlos during an air raid I heard two Marines talking about why they joined up: 'I was a baker's roundsman,' one said, 'but I kept fucking up the orders. One day I lost £300 of cream buns so before they could give me the sack I went off and joined the Marines. It's great, football twice a week, a few lectures. There's the odd yomp, but you usually finish up in the pub.'

All the men were fanatically clean and tidy. There were always lengthy queues in the *Canberra*'s laundry of soldiers ironing creases of geometric precision into their fatigues. They were friendly and cheerful too and courteous to a degree that was so at odds with the norm in the civilian world that we were always suspicious that our legs were being pulled.

We arrived at Freetown, Sierra Leone, on the morning of Saturday, 17 April, eight days after leaving Southampton. The bumboats that clustered round the hull within minutes of docking were greated with a shower of spit from the Marines hanging over the rails. The air was hot and wet. Freetown looked interesting in a seedy way, a collection of low, badly built houses thinning out as the land rose to form tawny hills swathed in scrubby vegetation. Someone remembered that Graham Greene had worked as an Army intelligence officer here in the war. The British consul came on board for a drink with the Captain. Apart from that the only sign of the British community of three or four thousand was some suntanned girls who came down to the jetty to wave to the troops who hung from the decks, radiating lust. No one was allowed ashore because, they said, of the risk of contracting malaria. It was a relief when the ship set sail again at midnight.

The next day, the ship was hit by a strange outbreak of superstition. Four days earlier we had hit a whale, killing it and staining the sea with blood, which some of the men took as a bad portent. A series of worrying coincidences followed. A story went around that a French clairvoyant had predicted that a great white whale would be sent to the bottom of the sea, plunging the world into a final war. The ship's nickname was the Great White Whale. Then it was noticed that the postal number given to the *Canberra* by the British Forces Post Office was 666, which as every soldier knew from the horror movie *Omen* showing on board, was the mark of The Beast of Revelations. The story produced near panic in some quarters. One padre tried to turn the rumour round by arguing jesuitically that the number meant not that we were doomed but that we were the agents of the Argentinians' destruction. The story was potent enough to help persuade some of the P & O crew and one of the journalists to leave the ship at Ascension. As the war got closer we would toast him every night in the bar: 'The only one of us with any sense.'

We sailed to Ascension through glorious blue seas. The sky broadened and high puff-balls of cloud appeared. Dolphins raced enthusiastically alongside either bow and flying fish flicked out of the swell. The mood on board was growing sombre, however, especially among the senior officers. As we came closer to the Falklands, they were beginning to revise their assessments of the Argentinian military competence and the size of the job awaiting the task force.

One night a senior officer said in the Crowsnest: 'This could be terrible, a disaster. We only have to lose one ship, or one company of men to set the military back years.' The journalists were feeling apprehensive too. The day before we arrived at Ascension the quartermaster of 42 Commando started selling kit and we queued in the sweltering heat to buy denim trousers and 'woolly pullys'.

Cross-decking: troops arriving by helicopter
on *Queen Elizabeth II*

**Bound for Blue Beach II
at San Carlos Bay**

**Air Alert Red:
a Gurkha awaits attack**

A captured 30mm anti-aircraft gun
used at Goose Green against
advancing Paras

Burial of Argentine victims
at Goose Green

Sir Galahad ablaze after Skyhawk bomb attack

Troops advancing against the background of Mount Harriet

Cool under fire: Guardsmen being shelled.
The white explosion is a round hitting
British phosporous grenades

Casevacced out in a Gazelle

Marines advancing

**White flag over Stanley: victorious Scots Guards
on top of Tumbledown**

'The para has a tremendous
capacity for violence.'
Paras in Port Stanley

Defeated army

Going home. Conscripts about to board *Canberra*

On Tuesday we dropped anchor a mile off the island. It looked like a Welsh slag heap transposed to the tropics. Ascension was constructed entirely out of horrid, dirty-looking pumice stone except for a single hill in the middle, the Green Mountain, which was high enough to be moistened by cloud and which grew enough vegetation for cows to graze and for there to be a bamboo grove around the fishpond that we were told was on top.

We were expecting to see a huge armada of warships in the anchorage. Instead there were only HMS *Fearless* and a few logistic ships, for the Grey Funnel Line, as the fleet was known to the Marines, had sailed two days before.

Fearless was the home of Brigadier Julian Thompson and Commodore Michael Clapp, who were jointly commanding the landing force. Their operations centre was the room where Ian Smith and Harold Wilson had met in 1966 for barren talks about the future of Rhodesia.

On Wednesday, 21 April, we went aboard for a briefing. Clapp said that eight options were being considered for the form the landing should take. They varied from a direct assault on Port Stanley to pin-prick raids that would be part of the tactics of a blockade. Other possibilities were a landing on West Falkland which would stay put, inviting the Argentinians to come to the task force, or a landing on East Falkland and an advance on the capital. Even at that early stage the latter seemed to make the most sense. Later that day I looked at a map for the best landing sites and chose the area around Foul Bay, slightly to the north of where we eventually went ashore.

Clapp and Thompson were surrounded by a team of advisers. The most important were the commanding officer of the SAS and a Marine Major, Ewan Southby-Tayliour. An amusing and mildly eccentric man, Southby-Tayliour was a godsend to the Brigadier. He had recently whiled away a tour of duty on the Falklands by sailing around every inch of the coastline, charting all the reefs, rocks and coves. The fruits of his research were distilled in a yachtsman's guide to the islands which he had written but was unable to get published because only two or three yachtsmen visited the Falklands in any year.

The SAS colonel's function was to direct his men so that their intelligence gathering activities on the Falklands were geared to the proposals that Thompson and Clapp had for the shape any landing should take. All projections and scenarios dreamed up on *Fearless* were sent back to the Fleet Headquarters at Northwood to be tested against the projections and scenarios of the planners there. We were told that at the end a short-list of possibilities would be put to Mrs Thatcher and she would choose, but in the end the plan was Julian Thompson's and effectively there was no other choice.

The next eleven days were spent in a perpetual state of anticipation of the move south. During the day there was constant activity with helicopters flying between ships, their nets bulging with supplies and ammunition. The troops were taken ashore in rotation to practise firing rifles, mortars and anti-tank weapons. The journalists were forbidden to set foot on the island. The reason, we assumed, was that the Ministry of Defence was worried about us seeing the American Starlifter transport planes which had been flying into Wideawake airport several days before the 30 April announcement that America would provide material aid to Britain. The evidence of American help, however, was already lying off our starboard side in the shape on an American Navy oiler that arrived two days before news broke of Reagan's decision.

For a day after we heard that South Georgia had been taken we had high hopes of moving off quickly, but instead of taking the conflict forward, the victory seemed to set everything in concrete. The week that followed was the dullest and most dispiriting of the campaign. Diplomacy creaked back into action. The pace slowed down and the decks were once again carpeted with troops 'bronzing' with all the dedication of secretaries on a fortnight in Torra del Mar.

During those slack days the behaviour of the ship was watched with increasing interest by the military medical team's psychologist. Early in the voyage he predicted that we would face an almost intolerable accumulation of psychological pressures the closer we got to conflict. Once the fighting started he predicted a heavy crop of battle-shock victims suffering nightmares, hallucinations and incontinence. In the event not one mental casualty was reported during the conflict, though some might have emerged later. His fame spread following an incident when a signaller, whose behaviour was causing alarm, was sent to him with a fake message so the psychologist could carry out a surreptitious examination. He asserted that the man was teetering on the brink of insanity. It emerged later that the signaller had handed the message to someone else to deliver and the psychologist had got the wrong man.

Perhaps as a result of the – to an outsider – irreconcilable contradictions of being dedicated to saving lives while being part of an organization dedicated to taking them, the medical men were in some ways the most uncomfortable group on board. They were an earnest lot, in contrast to the flippant fighting men, and extremely hawkish. One of the most bellicose was a surgeon. The *Standard* correspondent, Max Hastings, claimed he broke into the hospital refrigerator at night and drank the blood. We also suspected he was looking forward to the possibility of some experimental surgery when the fighting began.

Despite the renewed diplomatic activity, we felt in ever increasing danger. On Monday, 26 April, *Canberra* set sail at dusk and spent the night steaming round and round the island. An Argentine freighter, *Rio de la Plata*, had been watching the assault fleet for three days and there was a sudden alarm that she might be carrying divers who had attached limpet mines to the *Canberra*'s hull. The threat was taken seriously enough for the Navy to send divers down to check. After that we set sail every night and sometimes during the day. Watching the same dreary features of the island passing monotonously on the ship's rail every few hours deepened our frustration and quickened everyone's desire to get on with the fighting.

On Saturday, 1 May, I saw a Vulcan bomber coming in to land at Wideawake. A few hours later the BBC news announced that there had been a bombing raid on Port Stanley airfield and the runway had been cratered badly, aircraft destroyed and ammunition blown up. Later we saw the reconnaissance pictures, which the MOD decided sensibly not to release in London. They showed the bomb craters forming a neat X across the airstrip. On the runway proper, though, there was only a single hole. The many subsequent raids only managed to make one more crater. The attack, once again, started hopes that we would soon be away. The tedium was maddening. Every night we played reckless games of poker to avoid having to go to the bar.

At last on Monday, 3 May, we heard of a definite plan. We would be leaving within three or four days and sailing to the edge of the Total Exclusion Zone, outside the enemy's air range where some of the units would 'cross-deck' to warships. The landing would then follow within forty-eight hours. The question remained as to where the landing would be. There was still no certainty that the planners on *Fearless* had plumped for an unopposed landing and there was considerable alarm that political pressure for a swift result might push the landing force into a bloody direct attack on Port Stanley.

The Vulcan raid was followed by more news that had an initially cheering effect. At first we thought the sinking of the *Belgrano* was just the action that would teach the Argentinians the futility of carrying on their fight, especially as the first reports suggested that the submarine captain had deliberately aimed the torpedo to wreck the cruiser's steering gear, disabling the vessel but enabling the crew to escape. As the death toll climbed with each new bulletin attitudes changed from jubilation to embarrassment to defiance. 'What the fuck do you expect?' snapped a Marine lieutenant when I held forth about the damage this would do to Britain's case in world opinion. 'Are we meant to wait for the Argies to be nasty to us first until we're allowed to be nasty back?' But the incident left a sour memory. Military men revere rules. There was no escaping the realization that by sinking the *Belgrano* outside our own 200 mile zone we had made the rules and broken them.

Most of the senior officers thought the affair was regrettable, in particular Lt.-Col H. Jones, commanding officer of 2 Para, who had come on board at Ascension while he waited for the rest of his battalion to arrive on *Norland*. In the event we only had to wait a day to find out how nasty the Argentinians could get. On Tuesday, 4 May, the news came through about the *Sheffield*. It had the immediate effect of concentrating everyone's thoughts on the vulnerability of the *Canberra*. If the *Sheffield*, with her missiles and chaff could be sunk, how much more defenceless were we? H. Jones told everyone cheerfully that he was looking forward to getting off the ship. 'Sink this and the war is over,' he predicted.

The incident silenced the jingoes for a day or two. The Argies were clearly capable of fighting back. We set sail from Ascension on Thursday, 6 May, in a mood of foreboding. Last letters began to leave the ship. Journalists telexed their offices to find out what life insurance cover had been arranged for them. The following days brought a series of uncomfortable discoveries. We heard that one of the unit commanders had passed out when blood was mentioned in a first aid lecture. More seriously, the pretence that we could ever achieve air superiority over the Argentinians was slowly being abandoned. The admission was first made in a lecture on the sea war given by Commander Tim Yarker thirteen days before the landing, when he revealed that the 'air superiority' talked about at the intelligence briefings as essential before a landing could go ahead was going to be achieved by a gradual erosion of Argentinian aircraft in a series of air battles that would precede the amphibious assault. At an intelligence briefing a few days later given by 42 Commando's intelligence officer, Henk de Jeger, it became clear from reports sent back by SAS and SBS patrols on the islands that the Argentinians were alarmingly well-equipped. We heard for the first time they had at least one 155mm gun capable of firing half way across East Falkland. The biggest gun we had was the 105 which could propel a projectile only seventeen kilometres. They had an impressive array of anti-tank weapons to use against our six Scorpions and Scimitars, plus many tanks and Panhard armoured cars of their own.

After that, lectures given to the journalists on survival and first aid took on a new urgency. We were taught how to build stone sangars out of rocks and peat to protect ourselves from shell splinters and enemy bombs; how to dig slit trenches and shell scrapes to increase our chances of coming through a bombardment alive; and the importance of having eighteen inches of dirt above your head to stop the shrapnel from airburst bombs. Around the ship makeshift screens were pinned up for showing American medical training films. The narrator had a ghastly 'I speak your weight voice' in which he described the intricacies of how to deal with a sucking chest wound which, as the military joke went, was 'nature's way of telling you you have been in a firefight'.

As the weather worsened and the ship bucked and plunged through the force eight gales that blew up in the Roaring Forties, black masking tape began to appear on all the glass, and heavy furniture was lashed down to prevent it being thrown around by storms and blast. Through the streaming windows of the ship you could see the albatrosses skimming over the seas, trailing their wing tips in the crests of the waves. Those of us who had mocked the keep-fit fiends began lumbering round the deck in brand new DMS boots in a futile attempt to soften the unyielding uppers before we got ashore.

On Thursday, 13 May, the P&O crew were told the *Canberra* was going all the way to the Falklands and the kitchen boys, engine room crew and waiters were officially informed they were now liable to be pressed into service. As at every stage of the voyage they took this unexpected news well. Most had signed on for the money after spending up to a year hanging around in the unemployed seamen's pool waiting for work. The pay was good. Once the *Canberra* crossed the Equator all wages went up 150 per cent. Nevertheless this was not enough to compensate for the fact that the civilian crew was kept in the dark about almost every new development on the voyage. They were told originally they would go no farther than Ascension. Then that they would not be going into the 200 mile exclusion zone. Except for a handful who slipped ashore at Port Stanley none of them ever set foot on the Falkland Islands. Half the crew were enthusiastically heterosexual, and full of stories about their conquests on cruises. The remainder tended towards the camp. One of the laundry boys would time his entry into your cabin just as you had emerged naked from bed and make small talk as you tried to shave. The Marines did not appreciate his informal approach to ship life and he had to be locked into his cabin for his own protection after he was set upon by a bootie who he had surprised in the showers.

The first indications of the form an attack would take leaked out in the Crowsnest bar on Friday, 14 May, the day after the battalion commanders had been helicoptered to *Fearless* for an O(orders) group meeting with Brigadier Thompson and Commodore Clapp. The landing was to be on the beach around San Carlos Water. The SAS and SBS patrols reported there were few Argentinians in the area. The units would be going all the way on *Canberra* as far as San Carlos Water where they would be moved ashore in landing craft. Saturday, 14 May, brought some cheering news. The SAS had attacked an Argentine airbase on Pebble Island, north of West

Falkland and destroyed eleven aircraft, including six Pucaras. Even the fainthearted among us rejoiced. All that day the weather worsened steadily. As dusk fell some Marines went up to the ship's bridge wings to test fire four general purpose machine guns which they slotted into holes bored in the ship's rail as a token protection against the Argentinian Air Force. The pink tracer streamed out beautifully from the ship's sides and was whipped into arcs by the fifty knot wind howling across the waves.

When I got back inside there was a practice 'Air Alert Red' in progress. The lights were dimmed and the corridors were filled with silent, prone figures. It looked like a scene from a gothic horror film where the heroes board a drifting vessel and discover that some inexplicable calamity has overtaken the ship's company.

That night *Canberra* altered course to the east to avoid worse weather ahead. We woke the next day to the sound of Commander Tim Yarker announcing an Air Alert Yellow, meaning there was a threat of an Argentine air attack. It was the first time this warning system had been used in earnest. During the afternoon *The Deerhunter* was shown on the Crowsnest video. Everyone looked hard at the scene where Robert de Niro visits his legless comrade in the veteran's hospital.

The following day the ship was convulsed by a sudden change of plan. It was decided by the amphibious warfare commanders that the risks of having three battalions of the landing force going in to land on one hull were too great and that 3 Para and 40 Commando would be moved to other ships at least twenty-four hours before the attack. The conviviality in the bars that evening was broken by constant interruptions over the tannoy calling people away to organize the move.

Once the orders had been given, a curious mood of gaiety crept over the bar. A waiter called Guy who played the piano well sat down to rap out an archaic selection of Forces' favourites. Slowly the bar began to take on the look of a set from a morale-boosting Ealing studios picture, with subalterns who were born fifteen years after the war standing round the piano holding glasses and stumbling through the half-remembered words of 'The White Cliffs of Dover'. Later that night we were issued with our full kit; camouflage windproof smocks and trousers, a Bergen rucksack, a huge plastic poncho that doubled as the roof of a bivouac, and deformed looking mittens that had a single finger knitted into them so you could pull a trigger. Much earlier on we had discussed the rights and wrongs of wearing a uniform ashore. Surely to do so would increase your chances of getting shot or blown up, and we would be better off distinctively kitted out in civilian gear, such as the brightly coloured anoraks we had bought before coming on board. It had been gently pointed out to us by the Marines that to do so would merely transform us into excellent targets for the Argentinian snipers.

The following day we made our rendezvous with the rest of the task force fleet. I went up to the bridge wings. There was an eerie grey light and the sea was flat calm. There were ninety-five ships in the armada by now, ranging from the big dark slab of *Hermes* to little tugs like *Irishman* and *Yorkshireman*. It was a powerful scene, not so much for the spectacle of so many ships gathered in such a lonely corner of the ocean, but because it demonstrated a tremendous strength of will that made me feel for the first time during the voyage that we were bound to win.

42 Commando gathered in the ship's cinema that afternoon to hear their commanding officer. 'I'd like to share one or two thoughts with you,' he told them. 'The most sincere thing I want to say is that I wish each and every individual the best of luck in what's to come. One thing you can be quite sure of is that your training, your equipment and the leadership throughout this unit, and most important your own morale, is going to give you the best possible chance of coming through what lies ahead successfully. The enemy outnumbers us. He has a lot of modern effective equipment and should have been perfecting his defences over the last six weeks. . . The conscripts however are listless and apathetic and even refusing to carry out basic duties. If they do crack let the buggers surrender quickly. When I heard you singing your Malvinas song the other night I felt a small, fleeting moment of sympathy for those miserable spics over there.'

70

3

D Day

The *Canberra* arrived at the northern entrance to Falkland Sound at 3.26 gmt. It was a beautiful night. The Southern Cross glittered overhead and every few minutes a shooting star skidded across the sky. The sea was as flat as a slate and the stars lit up the round shoulders of the hills on either side of the Sound. All this beauty and calm could not have been more unwelcome to the task force. We had been praying for rough seas, driving rain and mist, anything that would help to mask the sonar 'signature' of the fleet from any lurking Argentinian submarines and blot out a radar signal that would give the Port Stanley garrison time to react. In fact they already knew we were there. A high flying Canberra bomber spotted the fleet shortly after it entered the Sound and radioed back to Stanley. By 7 p.m. British signal intelligence heard the Argentinian military network reporting there were suspected enemy landings along the coast ten kilometres north of Goose Green.

Why the Argentinians failed to react to the report remains one of the war's great mysteries. Their intelligence had already forecast that San Carlos was a likely landing site soon after the task force sailed, but General Menendez had ignored the reports. 'They only had to get half a regiment into the area and we would still be there now,' said an SAS man after the war was over. At Goose Green they had the men and the helicopters needed to shift a battalion up to the beach-head within half an hour of learning of the task force's arrival. It could have turned the landing into a disaster. The landing plan had been finalized aboard *Fearless* on the Sunday before D Day but the site had been decided weeks before we left Ascension.

Julian Thompson said later that he was 'never wild about San Carlos. It was too far away from where you had to end up, like attacking Cardiff by way of Barmouth. But no matter how many times you went around it like a dog sniffing around a lamp-post you always came back to it. We had to go there but I didn't like it.' In one way, its distance from Stanley was one of its attractions. The Argentine garrison, where most of the troops were concentrated, was fifty miles away and it would take them a while to move up a full scale counter-attack, giving the task force time to catch its breath and consolidate. It was also a sensible choice from a political point of view. The time it would take troops to get to the other side of the island left plenty of opportunity for diplomacy to be resurrected and an Argentinian surrender before a battle for the capital became necessary. But distance also worked against the task force. Apart from the logistical and physical sweat of having to travel across the island, the route was barred by a series of splendid natural defensive positions. San Carlos Water itself appealed to the planners because it was surrounded on nearly every side by land, which would shield the fleet from Exocet attacks while surrounding hills would make it difficult for the enemy air force. They would also provide an admirable site for the Rapier batteries. Finally Thompson and Clapp had been told there were few Argentinians there. The SAS and SBS, who had been patrolling the area for a week before the landing, reported there was a company of Argentinians on Fanning Head, a low promontory on the northern side of San Carlos Water. Apart from that the place was clear. Subsequent events proved this intelligence to be far from complete.

The date of D Day was finally decided five days before the landing. The battalion commanders flew to *Fearless* for Thompson and Clapp to tell them the details of the operation. The original plan was to start landing the troops very early on Friday morning so that everyone was ashore by 6.30 a.m. leaving four and a half hours of welcome darkness to dig in before the enemy air strikes began. The Navy, however, pleaded for a later landing. As it stood the plan required the fleet to arrive at Chanco Point, where the troops would disembark at midnight. This would mean that on the voyage there the Navy would be inside Argentinian air range for at least four hours of broad daylight. Terror of the Exocet made this a nightmarish prospect and Thompson needed little persuading to put back the landings by four hours, which resulted in the end in the last troops going ashore after dawn.

Thompson's plan had two phases. In the first the landing craft would take 40 Commando to San Carlos Settlement, a small collection of tin houses with about twenty-five inhabitants, while 45 Commando were landed a kilometre away across San Carlos Water at a derelict refrigeration plant at Ajax Bay. As there were only sixteen landing craft capable of holding about 1,000 men, the ships had to return to the fleet before the second phase could begin. In this, 3 Para were taken to Port San Carlos, a similar settlement a few kilometres to the north of San Carlos Settlement, while 2 Para were to land on the southern shore of the anchorage, and move straight up Sussex Mountain to protect the beach-head from a counter-attack by Argentinians at Goose Green. While the troops were going ashore the special forces planned noisy diversionary attacks around the islands designed to fool the defenders into thinking the landings were taking place elsewhere.

Providing there were no Argentinians waiting for the task force, Thompson expected to start moving the 105mm artillery batteries and air defences ashore at first light. It was hoped the beach-head would be comfortably ringed by Rapier missiles by dusk. The next priority was the building of a Harrier pad so the fighters could refuel and take off economically to patrol the skies above San Carlos. 5 Brigade, it was confidently predicted, would be ashore four days after D Day, allowing the Marines and Paras to push forward. The plan emphasized the campaign was going to move fast. 42 Commando, who were to be held in reserve on *Canberra* unless the landing ran into trouble, were told they would be attacking beyond the beach-head within twenty-four hours.

For all this to go as smoothly as it appeared in the *Fearless* briefing room, however, required a remarkable display of meekness from the Argentine Air Force. Right up to the day of the landing the belief persisted that the air threat would be sorted out within twenty-four hours. We could expect air attacks on the first day, the theory went, but the Argentinian losses would be so great that after that they would stay away.

At 4.10 on the morning of D Day, standing on the bridge of *Canberra*, we saw Fanning Head come up on the port side and beyond it the entrance to San Carlos Water. Through a star-scope night sight we could see the LCU and LCVP landing vessels clustering round the hulls of *Fearless* and *Stromness*, then later the men clambering down from the decks, and the boats disappearing silently into the inlet. There was nothing to show the Argentinians knew we were there. Among the officers on the bridge there was delight at how well it was going and much laughing and joking. At 4.37, however, HMS *Antrim*, lying eight miles away to the north, reported four fast moving 'contacts' had appeared on her radar. A few moments later, little pinpricks of red light started appearing on Fanning Head. We assumed they were signals from an SBS patrol who had landed there earlier armed with a loudspeaker and a Spanish-speaking Marine captain to try and persuade the 100 Argentinians to give themselves up. The tactic had obviously not worked because a few minutes after the lights appeared we heard the noise of small-arms fire followed by the flat double boom of *Antrim*'s 4.5 inch guns. As the shells landed Fanning Head was lit up like a firework display. After that the bombardment went on until dawn. Further noises of battle drifted to us from the south as the frigate HMS *Plymouth* began shelling Darwin and Goose Green under the guidance of an SAS team on the shore. Outside Darwin, an SAS raiding party started an extravagantly noisy raid, firing their weapons from all directions in the hope that the Argentinians would think they were under a full-scale attack.

40 Commando were the first to set foot on the Falklands. It was the most dramatic thing they did in the whole war. Once in the settlement they went around the houses waking up families and racing upstairs to check for Argentinians. There were none. To 40's chagrin they spent the rest of the war dug in around the settlement guarding against an attack from the rear. As a small compensation their commanding officer, Lt.-Col Malcolm Hunt, took the sur-

render of West Falkland and sent two companies to join the Welsh Guards for the final assault on Stanley. On the other side of the water 45 Commando landed without incident. Inevitably, though, the operation took longer than expected and the landing craft were nearly an hour late in heading back to the fleet.

D Day morning opened in clear hard sunshine. On the *Canberra* the ladies of the P&O crew strolled round the promenade deck to get their first view of the Falkland Islands, rather like inquisitive nineteenth-century memsahibs docking at Bombay. After six weeks without seeing any land, apart from the unappetizing volcanic rock at Ascension, East Falkland looked delightfully green and soft. It did not, however, look nearly as safe as we had imagined from studying the maps. Instead of rearing straight up out of the water as the contour lines suggested, the hills around San Carlos Water sloped gently into the sea, and were clearly not going to present enemy aircraft with much of a problem.

We had been enjoying the view for only ten minutes when the ship's tannoy announced an Air Alert Red. After all the dummy runs it had got to the point where it was almost inconceivable that a real Argentine plane would appear. Then suddenly we saw it, a Pucara whipping fast over a hill at the eastern end of the Water. We watched from the bridge with fascinated horror. 'Engage!' 'Engage!' roared Captain Christopher Burne. The GPMGs on the ship's side started pouring bullets at the plane. Something twinkled under its wings and a salvo of rockets streamed brightly down towards HMS *Argonaut*, stitching the water behind her stern. Judging from the boldness of his approach the pilot did not expect so many ships because he quickly swung away towards the shelter of the hills on the northern side of the Water, pursued by machine gun bullets, Blowpipe missiles and Sea Cats that exploded spectacularly but harmlessly behind him. The attack made everyone very animated and they described to each other what they had just seen. Their accounts were completely at odds with what I had just witnessed. Someone said that the Pucara had been shot down, which it plainly had not, at least not within *Canberra*'s field of vision. The incident confirmed that eye-witness reports of warfare should never be taken too seriously, especially if they involve the destruction of enemy planes.

Forty minutes later the jets arrived. This time the defences were better prepared and as soon as the Mirages and Skyhawks appeared they were met with a defensive barrage from the fleet. There could be no doubt that at least one of the attackers was hit, for we watched the jet explode in an orange fireball after being caught by a missile. After that the attacks came in thick and fast. Below decks the Marines and crewmen flattened themselves on the floors and sheltered behind barricades of tables, bracing themselves for the seemingly inevitable hit. It was better to be in the open. Inside the *Canberra* it was impossible to tell whether the whooshing and banging was defensive fire or the noise of a bomb smashing into the ship. Watching the attacks from the deck was more exhilarating than frightening. Any hope that I could report the war dispassionately vanished when I found myself cursing as an Argentinian Skyhawk pilot desperately twisted his plane to safety out of the path of a pursuing Sea Cat.

Before D Day I had had a mental picture of how the first air raids would look. I imagined standing on the deck with a pair of binoculars while in the skies above the few plucky Argentine pilots who had managed to get that far weaved frantically trying to dodge a posse of avenging Harriers. Occasionally, to cheers, a trail of smoke would appear from one of the Argentine planes and it would crash into the hillside. Instead not a single Harrier was to be seen. The Skyhawks and Mirages flashed in unmolested and though the missiles looked impressive, especially the Blowpipe which sent out a glowing melon-sized projectile which always just missed, they did not seem a satisfactory substitute. Throughout all this the P&O crew sat calmly below decks. In the kitchen the meals were prepared and the waiters served them up on the tables in the Pacific Restaurant as usual. Their coolness was in contrast to the behaviour of one Marine major I saw who whenever the Argentine planes arrived would fling himself on to the floor of a strongroom, slamming the door behind him.

The attacks took place with incredible rapidity. After moments of fearsome action, the bay was suddenly left calm and peaceful with ships bobbing at anchor beneath blue skies. Apart from the incessant clatter of helicopters and the busy little 'rigid raiders' skimming back and forth, one could have been in a Scottish loch. The war seemed a thousand miles away.

The Marines of 42 Commando were the only unit not ashore. To their enormous relief they heard just before 2 p.m. that they would be needed on the beach-head after all to back up 3 Para at Port San Carlos. 3 Para's arrival on the island had been marked by a series of minor disasters. The delay of the landing craft in getting back from delivering the first wave meant that by the time the troops were in the vessels and heading for shore, it was broad daylight. The first company was meant to land at Sandy Bay, a mile or so to the west of the settlement. But about 100 yards from the beach their landing craft ran aground. It spent some time manoeuvring while a soldier prodded the water with a pole testing the depth to see if it was possible to wade ashore. The water was far too deep. Eventually the vessel moved back along the beach until it reached a point where the men could splash on to dry land.

As 3 Para advanced towards the settlement they were met by men from the SBS who had been observing the area for days. They told the commanding officer, Hew Pike, there were no Argentinians in Port San Carlos. In fact there were forty-two of them in the settlement who had been there for at least a week and who were visited every day by a re-supply helicopter from Port Stanley. While the SBS were talking to Pike the Argentinians were pulling out fast. As they scrambled along the hill behind the creek at the back of the settlement they were surprised by two Gazelle helicopters, escorting a Sea King which was carrying an underslung load of mortar shells. Why the helicopters were flying so far ahead in an uncleared area was never explained. The Argentinians opened up on them with automatic rifles and sent the Gazelles crashing down. The two-man crew of one aircraft and the pilot of the other were killed. The Argentinians retreated along the bank of the San Carlos river and when 3 Para called for reinforcements were thought to be regrouping on the Knob, a little spur jutting into the river.

Back on *Fearless* it was decided to bring 42 Commando ashore and allow the Paras to go off in pursuit. The Marines mustered in the *Canberra*'s Atlantic restaurant. While we waited for the landing craft to arrive we smeared each others' faces and ears with dark camouflage cream. Then we filed through the kitchens past trays of hot sausages prepared for us by the *Canberra* cooks and out through the galley doors into the ships. The beach looked a long way away. The landing craft carrying Juliet and HQ companies set off at a depressingly slow pace as we watched the skies for signs of Argentine aircraft. A Marine pissed in the corner. They looked a terrifying bunch. The camouflage cream disguised their features, giving them an air of uniform menace. Their helmets were thickly covered with strips of sacking painted the colour of vegetation so that they resembled a gang of malevolent Jacks in the Green. We felt the scrape of the hull on the shore and the bow door fell open. It revealed a beach strewn with granite boulders and two sea birds which flapped unconcernedly out of the way. There were some groans. The bow door did not quite reach dry land so we had to wade through the freezing water. At close quarters the island looked just like the photographs which were pinned, for familiarization purposes, around the ship. There were no trees or even shrubs, just steepish hills covered with heather and rocks. Juliet Company fanned out and advanced towards the ridge ahead. HQ Company with Colonel Nick Vaux at their head moved off towards the distant buildings of Port San Carlos settlement gleaming in the cold afternoon sun. Looking back at the fleet moored in San Carlos Water you could see the helicopters buzzing back and forth between the ships and shore, taking advantage of the temporary lull in the air strikes.

Port San Carlos was a collection of square corrugated iron buildings, painted the cream and green of old Southern Railway stations. The houses were surrounded by a jumble of chicken coops, sheds and vegetable patches. It looked like a seedy corner of thirties outer London suburbia. The first door we came to was the home of Alan Miller, the farm manager. Round at the back they were handing out cups of minestrone soup to the newcomers. We talked to them for a bit. They had never doubted that the British Army would arrive some time so were not all that surprised to see the soldiers. They quickly lost interest in the subject of the invasion and one of them went on to ask if we had ever come across his son who lived in Illminster. The sound of gunfire and bombs started up again from the direction we had come from but the Falklanders chattered on without concern. It was the first of many peculiar displays of *sang froid* we were to witness from the islanders.

At first during the threat of air raids locals had dived under tables but they quickly became impervious to danger, wandering round with jugs of tea for the troops digging in all around. The only lull in activity came when a window was flung open by a radio operator to shout 'red'. Those nearby would repeat it and gradually everybody, or nearly everybody, realized there was an imminent air attack. There was no more formal system, not even a hooter or bell. The result was that someone might shout 'Fred' or another name and troops would dive for their trenches or dug-outs. There they would crouch, trying to avoid the puddles in the bottom, waiting for the air-burst bombs and machine gunning by Skyhawks and Mirages. But the planes rarely appeared – when they came it was invariably without warning – and after a few minutes the window would be flung open and the cry of 'yellow' would slowly carry around the settlement. Soldiers would clamber out of their holes, brushing off the dirt and shaking the water from their boots. Those who had not yet dug in would head for ditches, bales of wool or take refuge under a rickety jetty. If Argentine planes came into view everyone would open up with whatever weapon they could grab. Much of the shooting at long range was pointless and was more a form of boosting morale and testing guns.

By the time Nick Vaux had spoken to Hew Pike it was clear that 42 had not really been needed after all and the Argentinians had cleared off completely. The impression that the Argentinians might be preparing to fight had been created by the shooting down of the Gazelles. The first Gazelle to crash had ditched in the creek at the back of the settlement, badly injuring the pilot. The crewman managed to escape and free the pilot before the aircraft sank. He then swam with him to a buoy moored in the creek. While they were struggling through the water one of the Argentinians opened fire on them with an FN automatic rifle and continued firing until the pair were hauled ashore by people from the settlement living in a bunkhouse by the side of the creek. The pilot died a few minutes later on a couch in front of the bunkhouse fire.

The incident caused a lot of anger, not just against the Argentinians but also against whoever ordered the Sea King and its two Gazelle escorts forward to re-supply when the Paras had yet to signal that the area was safe. 'It was totally unnecessary,' said

Colonel Pike afterwards. 'One of the stupidities of war.' The surviving crewman stressed in his report how the episode had demonstrated once and for all how vulnerable Gazelles were to small-arms fire. For the remainder of the war the Gazelles acted mainly as air taxis for the battalion commanders and senior officers. Because they only had room for two in the back they were not even useful for moving patrols about, though in the final battles for Port Stanley they did a good and brave job as casevac transports flying into the firing line to pick up the wounded.

The Argentinians, meanwhile, seem to have been frightened at the repercussions of their actions for they fled in disarray and in all directions.

As dusk fell Juliet Company of 42, led by Major Mike Norman, the commander of the Marines who surrendered to the Argentinian invasion force at Port Stanley exactly seven weeks before, filed up to the hills beyond the settlement to spend the night patrolling. During the evening the story of the occupation began to emerge. According to two seventeen-year-old boys from the settlement, John Thain and his friend the son of Alan Miller the manager, the Argentinians had arrived a week before. There were forty-two of them and they told the local people they were there to set up observation posts. Miller's son spoke Spanish so he acted as an interpreter for his father and the Argentinian officer. The Argentinians expressed patriotic sentiments and said they were prepared to fight to the last man. 'They tried to get through to us that they were our friends and that they were here to liberate us,' said Miller. The troops set up home in the settlement's social club, a single storey wooden hut with a bar. When the Paras searched the place, moving gingerly for fear of booby traps, they discovered medals Mike Norman and his men had left behind in Port Stanley, though no one knew what they were doing there. According to the locals the invaders did not make very impressive soldiers. They drew their water from a sanitation ditch and seemed to live on sweets and boiled fish. Even so they were polite and well-behaved and listened to the inhabitants' complaints. One night Port San Carlos had one of its frequent power cuts and the Argentinians ran around in confusion thinking that the British attack had begun. When they fled during the real assault they left behind all their equipment including their sleeping bags, without which they would be lucky to survive more than a few nights in the open.

This account of a disorganized, ill-fed inefficient enemy matched the picture that had been painted of the Argentinians at the intelligence briefings, though it was to be refuted by much that we later saw. The account given by the local people was confirmed within a few days by three Argentine conscripts captured by the SBS on Fanning Head. They were flat-faced, harmless looking creatures, mestizos from the north of the country who had just finished their year of national service when the crisis blew up and who wanted only to go home. A nineteen-year-old called Miguel Garcia was the most talkative. He came from the village of Chavira and had ten brothers and sisters. He arrived in the islands by troop plane on 26 April. A week before his capture he was flown up to Fanning Head from Port Stanley but seemed to have little idea of what his unit was meant to be doing there. Garcia was in a patrol of twelve when they ran into a group of SBS men. When the SBS opened up, eight had fled and the remainder had all received identical rifle wounds in the thigh from Amalite rifles, which the SBS, like the SAS, preferred to the heavier standard issue SLR (self-loading rifle). At the time I spoke to him, in *Canberra*'s hospital, it seemed likely that he would lose his leg.

I spent that first evening in the settlement bunkhouse. It was a spacious building, constructed like almost everything on the Falklands out of sheet tin. It was home for half a dozen or so unmarried labourers who worked on the farm as shepherds, handymen and slaughterers. They were small, reserved men who spent the evening sitting silently in front of the peat fire, occasionally looking at one of the five-year-old *Reader's Digests* in the bunkhouse bookshelf or playing darts. The landlady, Mrs Thora Alazia, brewed huge pots of tea for the journalists and medics from 3 Para who had taken over the place as a regimental aid post and offered home-made ginger biscuits, helped by a pair of plump, giggly girls. We drank the tea in Silver Jubilee mugs, watched by a portrait of the Duke of Edinburgh that was pinned up on the wall. Everyone behaved as if it was a normal day apart from the arrival of some unexpected strangers. Mrs Alazia complained at how dull the place was getting. 'We usually have whist drives at the social club once a week. Sometimes we have a dance.' She looked thoughtfully out of the window. 'This year there's been nothing.' The gloom of the road outside was suddenly pierced by the lights of tanks travelling past.

Shortly after midnight, a small landing craft chugged into the creek. Two other journalists and I decided to hitch a ride on it back to the *Canberra* to ensure our dispatches got away. The sea had roughened and the angular shape of the hull bored into the waves drenching us with spray. As we approached the ship we could see troops disembarking. *Canberra* seemed deserted when we got on board. Apart from a handful of rear echelon cooks and quarter-master staff from 42 Commando all the troops had gone. I went up to the ship's hospital. The ward was full of survivors from HMS *Ardent* which had been abandoned that evening and had subsequently blown up after being pounded by Argentinian planes all day.

Sitting on the *Canberra* considering the landing it was hard to know whether it had gone well or badly. All the men were ashore safely but six frigates had been hit and only the fact that so many bombs had failed to explode that prevented an unimagined scale of carnage. The Argentinians had lost seventeen aircraft but they had still managed to get through the Combat Air Patrol twelve times. The most worrying element in the equation was the Argentine Air Force. No one had expected them to be so brave or so skilful. If they showed the same vigour in the following days it seemed possible that the fleet would all be sunk before the assault force supplies and equipment were moved ashore.

Looking at the *Canberra* from the shore it appeared miraculous that the Argentine planes could have missed her. She was at least twice the size of every other ship in the anchorage. Captured pilots later told the SAS that they were under orders to go for the warships rather than the transports, but bombing at speed with a curtain of missiles and bullets coming towards you is not an exact science and it seems incredible she escaped injury. The miracle was unlikely to be repeated. That night *Canberra* set sail to float in limbo for a while on the edge of the Total Exclusion Zone.

4

'Follow Me'

Looking down from the helicopter you could follow the progress of the battle from the scars on the ground below. Five miles outside Goose Green the hills flattened out into a featureless plain. The Argentine shells and mortars had gouged pretty stardust patterns into the peat that grew more frequent as the settlement approached.

We flew over the blackened wreckage of a Scout helicopter shot down by a Pucara. By the time we got to the airfield every ten yards of ground was churned into shell craters. Three Pucaras stood on the ground at odd angles, their fuselages crumpled by blast and sieved by shrapnel holes. It really looked like a battlefield, the only one of the war that lived up to expectations. Inside the settlement the sheepsheds were full of sleeping prisoners. The walls and roofs had already been painted with 'PoW' and its Spanish equivalent 'PG' to discourage the Argentinian pilots. Outside, sullen captives wandered through the mud carrying their weapons to the dumps. There were piles of ammunition and ordnance lying everywhere. A stack of brand-new Browning .5 heavy machine guns had not been taken out of their boxes.

The ground was littered with sodden clothing, helmets, sleeping bags and good luck cards from Argentinian school children exhorting the soldiers to fight to the death for the Malvinas. They were similar to the drawings sent to British troops, the kind of drawings found on noticeboards in primary schools or above the desks of proud parents.

Rifles stuck in the ground with helmets on top marked where men had died. Bodies were being collected by Argentine prisoners, hauled out by the legs and thrown into a tractor trailer where they were taken to a mass grave. A brief service on a blustery, wet day was conducted jointly by an English and Argentinian padre but as the water rose from the peat the bodies wrapped in drab green ponchos began to float. Only the boots sticking out from the burial shrouds showed that these pathetic bundles had once been human.

The scene at Goose Green was in total contrast to the spirit of caution that had ruled the task force's first week ashore. The air raids of D Day rattled the commanders and made them revise their opinion of the Argentinians' will and fighting ability. By D Day plus one there was a palpable air of restraint at Brigade Headquarters.

The calm of Saturday made the events of the previous twenty-four hours seem like a ghastly dream. Not a single Argentinian aircraft appeared in the sky above San Carlos Water and the helicopters buzzed back and forth from ship to beach-head with rations, equipment and ammunition. Away from the troops it could be remarkably quiet, with just the sound of the wind over the barren moor. The dull explosion of bedding mortars still caused men to jump and look for cover. No one could understand why the planes had not returned. The pilots had proved they could get through and sink ships. Why did they not press their advantage and smash the force before it had time to grow roots on the beach?

They certainly had the courage. 'I never thought I would say this,' Colonel Vaux, the CO of 42 Commando, told his officers. 'But I take my hat off to the Argentinian pilots. They really have been incredibly brave.' One of them, twenty-nine-year-old Ricardo Luccero was captured later in the week after ejecting from his Mirage over San Carlos Water. He smashed his knee while escaping from the cockpit and we saw him lying in the Ajax Bay field dressing centre alongside some badly burned survivors from HMS *Antelope*, being treated with a mixture of deference and curiosity. He said that those pilots who survived a sortie against the fleet were ordered not to return to their home base but to fly to another airfield in order the minimize the effect of the losses on morale.

Ajax Bay was the most depressing spot on a cheerless island. The dressing station was housed in a derelict crumbling concrete edifice that had once been a refrigeration plant for freezing sheep carcases. Over the door someone had painted: 'Welcome to the red and green living machine,' a reasonable boast for everyone who went into it alive survived. The air inside was hot and damp and smelled of medication and the floors were covered with rows of wounded men being attended to by unshaven and exhausted-looking medics. Lying in the middle of the Brigade maintenance area it was hit several times by Argentine bombs, one of which passed through the walls without exploding.

The breathing space only lasted twenty-four hours. On Sunday, wounds licked, the Skyhawks and Mirages returned. This time the Rapier batteries were in position and seven enemy planes were downed in the raids. They still managed to hit HMS *Antelope*, an elegant, 3,250-ton Amazon class frigate that had escorted *Canberra* for some of the way, and ironically entertained us with a demonstration firing of her anti-aircraft guns. The bomb that hit did not go off at first. The theory prevalent among the Navy to explain the number of duds the Argentinians were dropping was that the bombs were fused after the tail had spun a certain number of times on descent. The pilots were releasing them too low for them to go off. *Antelope*'s bomb exploded killing a naval expert who was attempting to disarm it and she sank, stern first, into San Carlos Water. By morning only her sharp prow remained visible, jutting from the waves like a cartoon representation of a shipwreck.

On Monday the jets were back again, and again the ships in the anchorage were blessed with some incredible luck. We watched the raids from the deck of the Royal Fleet Auxiliary *Resource*, an ammunition ship packed to the gunwhales with Sea Dart, Sea Cat and Sea Wolf missiles. It was a floating tinderbox. Unlike the warships, where all flammable materials had been stowed away, *Resource* had a wardroom like a Home Counties pub and was full of sofas, cushions and wood panelling. Two times out of three there was no warning that the Argentinians were coming. Two Skyhawks and a Mirage were the first in, flying so low that we were looking down on them when they flashed past fifty yards away. They turned at the end of the anchorage and came back for another run. The helicopters which had been criss-crossing between the ships rushed to the edge and flattened themselves against the hillside blending in with the vegetation. One pilot reappeared on *Resource* looking pale. A bullet had smashed through his windscreen and almost parted his hair. Groundfire from our own troops was always a danger and those in front of the guns had often to throw themselves to the ground to avoid being hit.

This time a Skyhawk lobbed a bomb in the direction of *Resource*. It plopped into the water fifty yards off her starboard side. As the planes roared away, clinging to the walls of San Carlos Water, the Rapiers pursued them. A thin line of smoke appeared from the back of two jets growing fatter and fatter as they dipped out of sight behind a ridge. The sound of an explosion just carried to us.

During the raids one of the ship's officers pointed at our life jackets and anti-flash gear. 'Why are you wearing that?' he asked. 'What you need on this ship is a fucking parachute.'

It was noticeable that once the pilots began their runs they let fly with everything they had, even dropping bombs on the uninhabited hills at the far end of the anchorage. Later we realized this had two purposes; first to lighten their load for the journey home, second to impress on their superiors back in Argentina they had put up a good fight. Once again we were depressed with the performance of the Blowpipes which crawled across the sky like a faulty Space Invaders machine where the blip never quite connects with the target. Thompson said the Blowpipe would be the first piece of kit to be 'binned' as a result of the war, and its likely replacement will be the lighter and more accurate Stinger surface-to-air missile carried by the SAS. Stinger proved itself on the morning of D Day, shooting down a Pucara sent up to San Carlos from Goose Green to see what was going on.

The Rapier teams led a solitary existence, perched high above the settlements, waiting for the planes to come. The missiles themselves were rather undistinguished considering their fearsome reputation and the amount of trust that was placed in them. There were four missiles to a unit, each about two and a half feet long and painted green with a yellow stripe down the side. At the battery above Port San Carlos the men had chalked on messages for the incoming pilots of the 'Fuck off Argies' sort. The sergeant explained that the missile had a range of 6.5 kilometres and travelled at mach 2. It carried only a pound of explosive, just enough to blast a hole in a plane. After three days ashore, however, he still hadn't downed an enemy plane: 'All I can say is that I was the first Englishman to fire a Rapier in anger in a war,' he said resignedly.

One night we chugged across the bay in one of the many camouflaged LCUs, the carthorses of the task force carrying men, equipment and vehicles ashore. At Brigade HQ the password that night was 'open house' and all along darkened paths we were challenged and heard the click as safety catches were released on hidden weapons. We spent a night with the Mountain Arctic Warfare Cadre, hardened mountaineers whose role was almost as shadowy as that of the special forces. With no sleeping bags that night we had to snuggle down between their bags in a tiny cottage warmed by a peat fire. Most of them were Scots; intelligent, observant men who had noted and approved the way islanders had come to terms with the environment. Hours before dawn we were woken from an uneasy sleep when someone kicked open the door and said: 'Get up. There's going to be an artillery bombardment on us from West Falkland at any minute.' We got dressed and waited. Nothing happened after half an hour. 'It did'na soond too likely,' one of them said and went back to sleep. The cadre woke us at daylight with hot porridge and coffee. They seemed able to conjure the most delicious food from the barest of ration packs and their generosity and kindness was unstinted.

During the air raids the momentum of the operation seeped away. Within forty-eight hours of landing, San Carlos Settlement was transmogrified from a staging post for Stanley into a garrison. The Marines of 40 Commando and Brigade, which had made its headquarters there, made themselves as comfortable as they could. Many set up home in a large red sheepshed, sleeping in the cribs and on huge bales of wool. Over at Port San Carlos 3 Para and 42 Commando lost no time in stamping their personality on the place. The ridge running down the south side of the settlement was honeycombed with elaborately constructed trenches, carefully camouflaged with slabs of peat. They moved into the bunkhouse and the social club formerly inhabited by the Argentinians. At the handsome home of Mr Miller, the settlement manager, the floors began to fill up at night, first with journalists, then with helicopter pilots and SBS men. Down at the sheepshed by the creek, every available corner was taken up by Marines. Within a few days the unmetalled track running through the settlement was churned into a thick river of mud by the tanks.

Despite the disruption, work continued and in the sheepshed the labourers from the bunkhouse stolidly slaughtered and skinned, seemingly oblivious to the change in circumstances. The paraphernalia of butchery deepened the already grim cheerlessness of our surroundings. Sheep heads littered the shore of Port San Carlos Creek. The settlements all over the island were dotted with gibbets hung with large hunks of nameless meat, curing in the cold sunlight.

By Monday night Colonel Vaux was telling the officers of 42 Commando that the Argentine air activity meant the battalion was staying put for the moment: 'There can't be any major operation outside the umbrella of our air defence,' he said. 'It would be far too risky.' Instead the priority was to continue getting supplies ashore and building up the beach-head. Resources were to be saved for SAS and SBS operations and raids. This caution pleased no one, though they accepted the reasoning behind it: 'I can see this developing into another Sebastopol with neither side knowing who is the besieger and who is the besieged,' said an officer.

The first raid was to be an attack on Goose Green by two companies of 2 Para on Monday night. The plan, devised by Colonel H. Jones, was in the words of a 2 Para officer to 'go down there, banjo the bastards, then beat it'.

The order to go ahead was given at 3 p.m. At 8 p.m., to H.'s fury, it was withdrawn. The brigadier decided that in view of intelligence reports that the Argentinians were reinforcing and because of the shortage of helicopters, the risk was too great. Two days later, although the situation had not altered substantially, 2 Para set off again, this time with the whole battalion. The reason for the change of heart, as even the lowliest soldier on the islands would tell you, was political.

On Tuesday, 27 May, the morale of the task force was probably lower than at any other point in the war. By then it had dawned on everyone that 5 Brigade's arrival was going to be delayed for days.

The 'air superiority' that had been a vital part of all the planning had still not been achieved and the weather was even more awful than anticipated. Finally the date could not be less auspicious. The 25 May was Argentina's national day and everyone expected General Galtieri to make a special effort to mark the occasion.

That evening we heard the results of that effort. The face of the radio monitor in 42's command post hardened first in concentration then creased into pain as the news came over the network that the *Coventry* and *Atlantic Conveyor* had been hit by Exocets. Once the report had sunk in a second realization dawned: the *Conveyor* was carrying three desperately needed Boeing Chinook helicopters, capable of lifting more than thirty men, a squadron of Wessex helicopters and spares for the Harriers. The prospect of any big push forward seemed to become even less likely. Thus, the news that 2 Para was going down to Goose Green in strength struck everyone as odd. For one thing there were the intelligence reports of men being moved into the garrison, albeit air force and administrative personnel.

In geographical terms, the Argentinians could scarcely have been on better ground. The approaches to Goose Green and Darwin included large areas of featureless ground that offered no cover to an advancing force. At one stage the land narrowed to an isthmus a couple of hundred yards wide that could be sown from shore to shore with mines, and if that was not enough the attackers would have to negotiate an easily defended ridge of land that straddled the terrain between the two settlements. 'A battalion should be able to hold off a division there for as long as it wants,' said one of the colonels.

Brigadier Thompson changed his mind after a telephone call to London on Wednesday, 26 May, made on the land force's secure communications satellite link at Ajax Bay. Whether it was Mrs Thatcher or the fleet HQ in Northwood which encouraged him to press ahead, none of the task force officers seemed to know. It was generally felt, though, that the purpose of the move was to wipe away the memory of the sinkings and restore the flagging momentum of the campaign with a fast, neat victory.

H. was jubilant. Late that night he led the battalion down from Sussex Mountain, following a track that led south to Darwin before forking east towards Port Stanley. The Paras decided to carry as much kit with them as they could so as not to be dependent on re-supply by the over-burdened helicopters. This meant a crucial decision on what to take and what to leave behind. H. decided that firepower was the important thing. They loaded up with as much belted machine gun ammunition as they could carry and took only two mortars and 300 bombs, for use in case they ran into trouble on the way to the 'start line' of the attack.

Later they were to regret not having taken more. The 'indirect fire' available to the Paras was painfully inadequate for a pitched battle. The battalion had also been allocated three 105mm guns and 1,000 shells to support the attack, which were flown into position at last light on the eve of the battle. A request for four Scorpion or Scimitar tanks from the Blues and Royals was refused. A staff officer at Brigade told the Paras they were needed for other tasks. When the battle started the Paras' lack of direct fire, which the tanks could have provided, was even more keenly felt than the mortar shortage.

Three hours before dawn on Thursday, D company arrived at Camilla Creek House, a small cluster of farm buildings several miles north-west of Darwin and found that the area was free of Argentinians. The battalion moved up to join them and hid among the buildings, snatching a few hours' sleep. At one o'clock they tuned in as usual to the BBC World Service news and to their astonishment heard the announcer say that Paratroopers were poised to attack Darwin. How the disclosure ever came to be made has still not been resolved but for the remainder of the war the BBC became an object of suspicion, bordering on abhorrence for the military. All the journalists felt the hot breath of their indignation.

The Paras now had no alternative but to dig in. 'We thought if they didn't know we were there by then they never would, so we got ourselves into defensive positions,' said the Para second-in-command, Major Chris Keeble, afterwards. The Argentinians, however, decided to stay put. Colonel H. pushed C Company forward to see what lay ahead. Their report confirmed SAS intelligence that about a platoon of Argentinians was holding Burntside House on the eastern side of the isthmus, while another platoon of about fifty men was dug in around a mound a few miles south and west. Behind them lay a further platoon. Their placing showed practical sense. They were, in effect, a sacrificial screen that would tell the commanders at the defences around Darwin and Goose Green the nature and direction of the British attack. Even at this stage the Paras believed there was only a battalion of fighting men in front of them, which would make it a one-to-one fight. These were not the odds recommended in the training manuals where a three-to-one balance in favour of the attackers is considered essential. To help matters, Colonel H. called in a Harrier strike to 'brass up' the enemy positions. Two jets attacked Burntside House, but while flying away over Goose Green one of them was shot down by anti-aircraft fire.

Later in the day, the Argentinians finally decided to react. A four-man patrol set off in a civilian Land Rover from Burntside House to see what was going on. They were intercepted by a group of Paras who shot the commander and took the rest prisoner. The Paras were encouraged by the sight of them. 'One of them was a great fat bugger and none of them had machine guns,' an officer said later. Helped by intelligence gleaned from the hapless Argentinian captives, H. drew up his plan. It was a complicated affair, divided into six stages. He decided to stagger the attacks so that in each action of the initial part of the fight there were three times as many attackers as there were defenders. The essence of the strategy was momentum. The Paras would have to move fast and keep up a heavy rate of fire. The BBC reporter, Robert Fox, who stayed with the Paras throughout the battle described the principle as being 'rather like an old-fashioned cavalry charge. This risks high casualties but it is the momentum that carries through the attack.'

H. decided to control the operation from the front. The darkness and the lack of detailed intelligence made it vital for him to be on the spot to react quickly to the battle's shifts of tempo and to minimize the confusion that a more conventional behind-the-lines chain of command might have produced. Prudently, he left a duplicate tactical HQ in the rear commanded by Major Keeble to take over if he was killed. Early on Friday, 28 May, HMS *Arrow*, a type-21 frigate, lying out in Falkland Sound, began the action firing 4.5 inch shells into the Argentine positions. The bombardment was short-lived. After two hours the gun jammed and the gunners were forced to begin using their limited supplies of artillery shells to keep up the direct fire.

The Paras' first objective was the platoon at Burntside House. At 6.30, in complete darkness, A Company under Major Dare Farrar-Hockley attacked the building. The Argentinians defended hard, but the three-to-one imbalance in the numbers and the Paras' superior firepower overwhelmed them. As a matter of policy the battalion was carrying fifty-six general purpose machine guns (GPMGs), twice as many as any other unit in the Falklands. It was hardly a very sophisticated weapon, little different from the Bren guns of World War II, but it was manoeuvrable and accurate and fired heavy bullets fast. 'The ability to create violence in 2 Para is considerable,' said Major Keeble afterwards. Most of the Argentinian defenders were killed or wounded in the attack. Half an hour later B Company moved in against the platoon holding the mound to the west of Burntside killing twenty-four of them. The few who managed to escape from both the encounters were hunted down by D Company and twenty more died in the mopping up.

The first phase of the battle had gone well. Colonel H. calculated that about a company of the defenders had been 'taken out' and there were three more remaining. To carry the attack forward he moved A Company on towards Darwin and B Company down to the defended ridge that ran west across the isthmus from Darwin Hill, which dominated the settlement. It was here that things began to go wrong. By now the Paras had run out of mortar ammunition and were fast running out of darkness. The enemy was cleverly dug in along the ridge in interlocking trenches designed so that each position was covered by the sweep of machine guns in the flanking bunkers. By now the Argentinian gunners and mortar men had got their range and were raking the ground over which the Paras were advancing with shells and bombs. To make matters worse, A Company were low on ammunition and at one stage of the battle ran out completely.

The Argentinians, however, looked secure. Contrary to intelligence reports, they had built their trenches with overhead cover to protect them from air attack. It was an unnecessary precaution as it turned out because for most of the day thick cloud cover prevented the Harriers from getting to the battlefield.

By first light, Colonel H.'s TAC HQ was so far forward that it had joined up with A Company whose progress had now slowed to a near standstill below Darwin Hill. There was little cover and the lack of artillery fire meant that instead of shelling the Argentinians off their positions, each trench would have to be taken piecemeal. This required a small group of attackers creeping along the dead ground until they were close enough to fire a 66mm rocket or a machine gun into the defences. The Colonel believed it was only a matter of time before the Argentinians at Goose Green moved up reinforcements to strengthen the ridge. Rather than wait until D Company arrived he decided to gather the men he had around him and throw them at the defenders' positions. By now they were below some Argentinian trenches dug into the sides of a dip in the front slope of Darwin Hill. He divided the group into two. His adjutant, Captain David Wood, set off with twelve men towards an Argentinian machine gun post. The attack was beaten back and Wood was shot dead.

The second group hurled phosphorus grenades to mask their attack and ran forward towards the guns. Sergeant Barry Norman was behind the Colonel as they went in: 'The smoke ran out and we were caught there, about thirty of us, along the top of the hill pinned down by quite heavy fire and in fact Captain Dent was killed in that part of the action. The CO shouted out "follow me" and turned to his right and down into the dead ground to the right side of the hill and headed towards the enemy position. I immediately followed and as I proceeded to follow him someone to my rear shouted "Watch out. There's an enemy position on the left." I looked left and saw an enemy trench and just as I noticed it they opened fire on me. I hit the ground and when I looked up the Colonel was between two enemy positions in completely dead ground. I returned fire to the enemy trench and the Colonel took his magazine, re-loaded it, cocked his weapon and went up the hill to the enemy position. As he got within three feet of the enemy position I shouted out "Watch your fucking back" but he took no notice and subsequently was shot in the back by a trench to the rear.'

In fact Colonel Jones had been shot in the neck and died almost immediately. As an operation it was a failure. Instead of tipping the balance of the conflict as he had hoped, 2 Para were now in even worse trouble. Over on the other side of the isthmus an Argentine company dug in around Boca House, a ruined homestead, had allowed B Company to advance over a lightly defended part of the ridge and on to the forward slope. Once they were established there, they opened up on them with machine guns and mortars. To add to the confusion, Pucaras had appeared, and a Scout helicopter flying ammunition up to the front line was shot down. Faced with the slow moving, piston-engined Pucaras, the Blowpipes were effective for once and managed to destroy one that was attacking a mortar position.

At that stage of the battle the Paras had the choice of pulling out or pressing on to possible annihilation. Major Keeble, now in command, consulted as best he could with his company commanders over the radio. Then he ordered A Company back into the attack against Darwin Hill and pulled B Company off their exposed position on the ridge's forward face and back on to the reverse slope where they were joined by men from the battalion's support company who had been waiting back at the start line in reserve.

Meanwhile D Company in an extraordinary feat of stealth, crept round the side of the west end of the ridge and along a ledge that hid them from the Argentine positions around Boca House, sometimes coming within ten yards of the defenders. By this time the British 105mm light guns were firing again. They laid down a heavy bombardment on the ridge while the infantry pressed forward. They were now equipped with Milan anti-tank missiles, brought up by the support company. Their use, according to Keeble, proved to be the battle-winning tactic. They were designed to knock out tanks using a seemingly infallible guidance system that required the operator to get the target in a sight on the firing post then press a button. Provided the target stayed within the cross hairs for the duration of the missile's flight it was almost impossible to miss. Against the Argentine trenches they had a devastating effect, and were later used with great success in infantry attacks throughout the campaign.

By now D Company had formed up to attack the Argentinians at Boca House. Faced with the sight of A Company who had now appeared on top of the ridge, their fire slackened. Soon white flags began to appear and the trenches emptied. By now it was 3.30 in the afternoon. The Paras had been fighting hard for nine hours. Ammunition had almost run out and they had still not encountered the main Argentinian force. Keeble decided to keep going. A Company, who had fired the first shot in the battle, were moved forward once again and reinforced with fresh troops from C Company who had been holding the battalion's rear. Their objective was a schoolhouse a kilometre north of Goose Green. In order to multiply the garrison's troubles, Keeble ordered D Company to move round in an arc to attack the settlement through the airfield lying to the west, and B Company to swing right round and attack the Argentinians from the south. As the Paras moved towards the airfield the Argentinians lowered a battery of six anti-aircraft guns and fired straight into them. Two radar-controlled Erlikon guns sited at the far tip of the settlement meanwhile pounded the northern approaches.

When A Company arrived at the schoolhouse they found the Argentinians were still full of aggression. In the firefight fifty of the defenders were killed before a white flag appeared. Some men from D Company, who had moved across to back up the attack went forward to take the surrender. As they walked across to them they were fired on from one of the trenches and the section commander and a soldier were killed. It seems unlikely this was a deliberate tactic and the surrender had probably not been fully agreed among the defenders before the flag went up. The incident resulted in orders to disregard white flags in future unless told otherwise.

An hour before dusk the fog finally lifted enough for the Harriers to get in. They flew low over the land, seeing off a few Argentine Skyhawks which had belatedly appeared to help with the defence. With surgical precision the Harriers bombed the artillery and anti-aircraft positions clustered around the east end of the settlement. Major Keeble watched them from Darwin Hill. 'Psychologically it shook up the defence terribly,' he said. 'The machine guns were silenced and suddenly the whole pace of the battle slowed down as the light faded.'

As night fell it started to snow. Helicopters took the chance of the lull to fly around the battlefield picking up the wounded. Major Keeble took stock. A Para patrol that had gone into Darwin to liberate the civilians had been told the Argentinians were holding

112 people in the hall in Goose Green. This ruled out the possibility of an artillery bombardment to shell the Argentinians into submission. He was reluctant to do so in any case because he felt that heavy casualties might risk a repeat of the damage to world opinion that followed the sinking of the *Belgrano*. Before anything was decided, though, his men would have to sleep. He ordered the British guns to stop firing in the hope that the Argentinians would also welcome a respite. The garrison accepted the gesture and the battlefield was silent for the first time in fourteen hours. But while the Paras took it in turns the rest, Keeble prepared a plan for a renewed attack the following day.

On Saturday morning Brigade Headquarters back at the beachhead received an offer from Alan Miller at Port San Carlos to try and contact Eric Goss, the manager at Goose Green, using the citizen's band radio network. Goss was asked to speak to the Argentinian commander, Air Vice Commodore Wilson Pedroso, to tell him two captured NCOs would be sent to him with a proposition from the Paras. Either the Argentinians were prepared to talk about a surrender or they must accept a state of siege. In either case, Keeble argued, the Geneva Convention demanded the release of the imprisoned civilians.

The NCOs set off towards the settlement. Their reappearance would signal the Argentinians' willingness to talk about a surrender. Careful to the last, Keeble radioed Brigade HQ to ask for three more guns, 2,000 high explosive shells and as many Harriers as were available to provide a persuasive demonstration of firepower on empty ground close to the settlement should the Argentinians decide to fight on.

But the Argentinian prisoners came back. Keeble rounded up the only fluent Spanish speaker in the force, a Marine Captain called Rod Bell, Major Tony Rice, the battery commander, a brigade liaison officer and two journalists, Robert Fox from the BBC and David Norris of the *Daily Mail*, to act as civilian witnesses, and they went down to the appointed meeting place at the settlement flagpole.

Speaking through Bell, the son of a British diplomat who had Spanish as his first language, Keeble told Pedroso that the first action must be for the civilians to be freed. The Argentinians agreed to this and explained the pre-condition of their surrender: the garrison must be allowed to submit with dignity. Keeble was sceptical: surely they must want more? But the importance of honour to the Argentinians was explained to him and he allowed the ceremony. Pedroso and his officers retired and re-emerged with 150 men who formed up in a hollow square. It was clear that none of them were fighting soldiers but administrative personnel and air force men. Keeble demanded to know where the troops were. Pedroso led him away and pointed down at the settlement. 'To my utter astonishment,' he recalled later, 'there were about 1,000 soldiers marching up the hill. I had no idea there were so many. It made us hold our breath. What if they had decided not to surrender?' The Argentinians threw down their weapons, sang the national anthem and it was all over.

Understandably the aftermath of the battle produced a view that the victory was mainly of Colonel Jones's making. But for the bulk of the fighting, and at the stages when disaster was closest, the Paras were led by Major Keeble. Colonel Jones's biggest contribution was the initial plan and the leadership he displayed which set the tone of the action. The manner of his death provided an emotional charge which propelled the Paras forward and eradicated any thought of retreat, though at times it seemed the only sensible thing to do. It established a standard of bravery that the rest of the competitive military struggled to match throughout the war.

Even at the time the circumstances of H.'s death struck many people as extraordinary. Attacking machine gun posts is the sort of job given to a subaltern, senior NCO and a few men. Some Marine officers wondered whether Colonel Jones was not involved in a private test of his own 'bottle'. From his record, however, the action was characteristic. Frequently in mock battles the Colonel had been judged to be dead by the umpires at an early stage of the proceedings. When the battalion went on exercise in Kenya before Christmas he had lost points for leading from the front.

Colonel Jones had an independence of spirit rare in the military. He was an old Etonian from a West Country landowning family and came to the Paras from the Devon and Dorsets. One of the parachute regiment's odder traditions is for newcomers to be treated as social lepers for their first few months. On his first day, H. roared up to the windows of the officers' mess in a vintage Bentley while they were drinking their coffee after lunch and the surprise this created caused the convention to be forgotten. The small dealings the press had with him created the impression of an argumentative, amusing man who grew exasperated with those who could not keep up with him mentally. On the way down to Goose Green he seemed to prefer the company of those out of the orbit of his command, notably Robert Fox and Major Rice, the battery commander attached to 2 Para. Corporal Beresford, the Colonel's driver, said about him after his death: 'He always led from the front and never had anybody do anything which he couldn't do himself. He was actually a very, very intelligent man as well as being very brave. He was very close to everybody and they all respected his judgement and I think everybody was quite happy to follow him to the end.'

In retrospect the importance of Goose Green will probably be regarded as psychological more than strictly military. Everyone cheered up tremendously after the victory as it seemed to provide a guide to the opposition's fighting force. The pattern of the battle suggested the Argentinians would fight well as long as they had the advantage, but faced with the prospect of heavy casualties, or even an equally matched fight, they would give in. A battalion had defeated 1,400 men. The garrison which had scarcely come under fire had surrendered to a plainly exhausted force half their size. The victory made the planners more audacious and broke the creeping inaction created by the air attacks and the bad news from the fleet. The Argentine military reputation, puffed up by the successes in the air, shrank back to the modest proportions it was assumed to have when 3 Brigade's strategy was being mapped. The value of the victory was in direct proportion to the detriment to the task force's fortunes if the Paras had lost. A defeat may well have lengthened the campaign by months.

The benefit of the battle in tactical terms is harder to divine. The Argentinian garrison at Goose Green was seen by the Brigade as a 'strategic reserve' but could it ever have seriously threatened the British advance? 'I still don't really think the attack was necessary,' said a senior SAS officer afterwards. 'It tidied up the plot nicely but they were never a real problem to us down there. They didn't have the helicopters to move up to the beach-head in sufficient numbers to harm us once we were all ashore and we could have pinned down their advance with a company.'

On the day that Goose Green fell, Maj.-Gen. Jeremy Moore, the land forces commander on the Falklands, came ashore. The purpose, he said later, was to take the political weight off Brigadier Thompson's shoulders. He saw another lesson in Goose Green. The lack of artillery, naval gunfire and mortar support had almost jeopardized the whole enterprise. When the final push for Stanley came it would only be when every piece of artillery and ammunition the task force had available was in place. The defeat also had a devastating psychological effect on the Argentinians. It convinced General Mario Menendez, the military governor of the Falklands, that losing was inevitable. On the day of the surrender British signals intelligence intercepted a message sent from Port Stanley garrison to Buenos Aires warning Galtieri to prepare for defeat.

5

Life on the Mountains

While 2 Para were moving towards Goose Green, Thompson ordered 3 Para and 45 Commando to push north. The plan was for the Commandoes to go to Douglas, a remote settlement by the side of a creek, and then for the Paras to move through them and on to Teal Inlet, half way to Port Stanley. There were no helicopters available so they would have to walk all the way. The Marines set off first. After they had gone the Paras' commanding officer, Hew Pike, began to doubt the wisdom of going to Teal Inlet via Douglas for it meant marching a dog leg. It was hard to see the point in going to Douglas at all. It was miles north of the direct route to Stanley and had no discernible strategic value. Colonel Pike consulted Alan Miller who pointed out a short and simple way to Teal, used by the locals. The Brigadier agreed the Paras could follow it.

The Marines call marching 'yomping' and they take a strange pleasure in it. 45 Commando regarded their great yomp north as almost a prouder achievement than their activities on the battle-field. They set off carrying packs that weighed up to 120 pounds, about the weight of a teenage boy, and followed a route that took them up and down hills, along rocky valleys and through stone runs of jagged granite that could stretch for a mile. When they came to rivers they waded straight through them. The *Sunday Telegraph* correspondent Charles Laurence marched with the Marines all the way. 'It was unbelievably hard work,' he said. 'It started off like a country walk at a good steady pace but after three or four miles uphill over rocks, then through bogs, I was shattered. I was only carrying a modest pack but it pulled at my shoulders and my boots were sodden. The weather was appalling – sleet, rain, snow, wind – and the terrain meant you could never get into your stride.'

The Marines ended up yomping sixty miles to the site of their first battle on the Two Sisters Mountain.

The Paras call the same activity 'tabbing'. They left Port San Carlos on 27 May, and marched continuously for twenty-four hours stopping occasionally to brew up some tea. Nine kilometres north of Teal they stopped for a rest during the day, lying low in case there were any Pucaras. The following morning, before dawn, they were there. They had done the journey, mostly by night and over rocks and bogs, in less than a third of the time Brigade predicted it would take them. Some of the first Paras to arrive at the settlement were greeted by the islanders in Spanish. There were no Argentinians there when they arrived but some were later taken captive in the surrounding area. They included an observation team who had been sent up there from Stanley without any radio or maps. The Paras pushed on straight away, picking up more prisoners as they went and by 1 June had reached Estancia House. Things were going so well that Colonel Pike decided to keep the battalion going. They moved across the river and on to some mountains on the east side that when climbed gave the Paras their first view of Stanley and the airport. All around there were abandoned Argentine positions littered with kit. The view was blocked by the bulk of their next objective – Mount Longdon. Two companies were pushed forward to set up bases from where they could patrol the approaches to the mountain.

As they reached the open ground below Mount Kent shells started falling around them. Sitting on Mount Longdon, the Argentinians could see the Paras advancing and had called down artillery fire. Having come this far the Paras were keen to keep moving, encouraged by a determination not to be outdone by 2 Para. When Brigadier Thompson heard how far ahead the Paras had got he signalled Pike immediately. 'I am concerned that you are pressing ahead too fast,' said the message. 'I do not want you to get into a position you cannot get out of . . . stay where you are and dig in.' The Paras moved into some cover and stopped for a while.

42 Commando were kept on at Port San Carlos for a few days after the Paras moved on, to secure the rear. There was a feeling at Brigade, possibly backed up by intelligence reports, that the Argentinians were planning to drop men into West Falkland to harass the beach-head from behind and possibly even parachute a force straight on to it.

On Saturday Nick Vaux told his officers they would be attacking Mount Kent that night. A long, high feature, it lies in the centre of the island, looking down on all the landward approaches to Port Stanley. The helicopter shortage had eased by now so the Marines would be flying straight up there.

The attack was pretty straightforward. They would move at night, set up base below the mountain then send a couple of companies in to clear away the Argentinians. By first light the following day they were expected to be on top, firing down on the Argentinians positions on Mount Challenger, across the valley. No one was sure how many Argentinians there were on the mountain, but it seemed the Marines could expect a serious fight. The opposition sounded careless from the reports of the SAS patrols who had seen them lighting fires, something a British soldier would never do for fear of giving away his position.

The news that the attack was going ahead had the effect of making everyone excited but anxious at the same time. The unit had gone over to central feeding by now so everyone gathered in the sheepshed by the creek for their last meal before going up the mountain. There was a special treat to go with the corned beef and diced vegetables, a powerfully sweet suet and apple pudding which everyone was enraptured by. One of the lieutenants was white with nerves. 'There could be hundreds of them up there,' he whispered. 'We could all be killed.' There was an hour or two to go before the helicopters were due. People wrote last letters on the free Forces airmail letters that were always lying around.

In the wooden hut where they slept, the officers dressed themselves with slow ritual, like matadors before a bullfight: long johns, vests, thick socks, shirts, quilted 'Mao' jackets and trousers and camouflage windproofs. Then they anointed their faces and ears with camouflage cream supplied by Max Factor and, still sitting, struggled into their packs. These were so heavy they had to take it in turns to haul each other to their feet, like mediaeval knights before a joust. Someone who was staying behind said: 'Can I have your binos if you don't come back?'

The helicopters took off late and an hour later they were back again. It was snowing so hard on the mountain they could not land. The next night they tried again. This time the weather was better. When the Marines arrived they found that all the Argentinians had gone. I went up to join them later. We left San Carlos in a relay of Sea Kings threading up the valleys to avoid attracting fire from enemy ground patrols. When the helicopter had staggered to the ground the fifteen Marines jumped out and formed a circle around it with their rifles at the ready. It was a clear moonlit night. A hundred yards away the Commando sentries were outlined against the sky. They were dug in around a rocky outcrop which provided a defilade from the Argentine guns at Port Stanley which had been shelling the area in a rather haphazard way earlier on.

We bedded down in sleeping bags covered with waterproof ponchos and hoped that the weather would hold, but a few hours before dawn it started pouring with the delicate drenching rain that you only seem to find on the Falklands, and by the morning everything was wet. Twice in the night we were woken by gunfire. The first time it was outgoing fire from a 105mm battery sited on the southern slope of the mountain. It had been in position for twenty-four hours and if high explosive shells were used, was just within range of the old Marine Barracks at Moody Brook, on the outskirts of Stanley, seventeen miles away. The second time it was machine gun fire interspersed with rocket explosions. In the morning I discovered the cause. An SBS patrol and an SAS patrol had wandered into each other and in the exchange of fire the SBS commander was killed. The SBS had been three kilometres out of their area when the clash happened. 'Bumps' or 'friendly-friendlys', as the military called them, were a frequent and unreported aspect of the war. Within a few days of getting ashore, two patrols from A Company and C Company of 3 Para 'bumped' near Port San Carlos. In the ensuing firefight nine of them were shot, two through the head, but astonishingly they all survived. One came home to a hero's welcome from the local paper who ascribed his injuries to a fierce encounter with the Argentinians. Quite late in the campaign two patrols from 45 Commando clashed and four men were killed. In every case this disaster happened when one patrol wandered into another's area. It was inevitable, given the dark and monotony of the terrain, but at the start there was only a primitive challenge procedure to identify friend or foe, involving calling out a password and waiting for the correct reply. Over long distances this was impractical, especially if you did not want to reveal your position. In the end the soldiers were told to fire a flare if they were in doubt. If there was an answering flare they knew the shapes ahead were friendly. Knowing that the night was full of trigger-happy Marines and Paras made wandering around in the dark a frightening business, especially as there was often doubt about what was the current password. It became worse when they changed from words to numbers, where the challenger would shout a figure and you had to reply with another figure to make up the code-number of the night, especially if your arithmetic was shaky.

That first morning on Mount Kent was warm by Falklands' standards; about three degrees above freezing, but the cloud had descended and there was a dense drizzle. Around the camp the Marines were putting the final touches to their bivouacs. These were ingenious constructions. The idea was to dig a little into the peat, not too deep or the hole would fill up with water, then build up the sides with rocks. It was particularly effective to rip up the Falkland heather and make a mattress, providing both comfort and insulation. A poncho was stretched over the top and the whole 'bivvy' covered with peat blocks to camouflage it. After a time they grew more and more grandiose as people improved and extended, like suburban DIY enthusiasts.

Little groups were crouched over solid fuel hexamine stoves, brewing up the first 'wet' of the day and preparing breakfast. There were two sorts of rations. They came in square cardboard packs the size of shoe-boxes. The first type had tins, usually chicken curry and an unpleasant fat-caked compound called a baconburger. There were occasional variations like spaghetti or steak and kidney pudding which were eagerly sought after. They were quite edible, but bland, and inevitably monotonous, although there were four 'menus', A, B, C, and D. The most popular were the Arctic 'rat packs', full of silver foil packets of powder that swelled up when soaked in hot water to quite tasty representations of beef curry and apple flakes. The best thing in them was the porridge, especially if you followed the Marines' example and mixed in chocolate powder, dried milk and pulverized biscuits to produce 'combat porridge', a calorie-laden mess guaranteed to kick-start any bootie into life at the beginning of the day. Both types came with a cellophane bag of 'nutty', the soldiers' term for sweets and biscuits. Men sucked Rolos and Spangles constantly, particularly during moments of fear.

Despite the dismal weather, their sopping sleeping bags and kit, and their austere surroundings, everyone on the mountain seemed incredibly cheerful. 'Sorry about the dreadful weather,' said Colonel Vaux, looking happier than at any time since the landing. 'It's been beautiful up until now.' The Argentine troops who had occupied Mount Kent and the surrounding high ground appeared to have melted back to Port Stanley at the sound of the first British helicopter, for the Marines had found mounds of dumped equipment. Over to the north you could just make out small figures on the side of the hills, men from 3 Para and 45 Commando. Several miles to the south and east was our next destination, Mount Challenger. L Company had moved up there the day before and we were joining them with a load of Milan missiles for use in the forthcoming attack on Mount Harriet. The troops set off in single file, balancing their kit on their heads like native bearers.

It took two and a half hours to cover four kilometres. We stumbled through boggy heather and clambered over hundred yard wide stone runs that looked eerie, like monastic ruins, in the mist. Occasionally the blanket silence was broken by the 'boom . . . whoosh' of our artillery firing towards Port Stanley. Later the noise was reversed. The Argentinians were firing back, harmlessly it later turned out, on to the unoccupied slopes of Mount Kent.

After a final haul up a long slope we were there, soaked in mist and sweat. The nylon tights we wore to keep us warm at night had you glowing after a hundred yards. After walking a mile steam seeped out of the top of your boots. The section delivered the missiles and set off back to Mount Kent. On the way we passed a group of men wearing pea-green waterproofs and carrying curious looking rifles with a second, fat, underslung barrel. They had longer hair then the other soldiers and some of them wore droopy desper ado moustaches. It was the SAS, one of several patrols we had seen that day. By this stage in the war, most of their important work was done.

Long before the SAS arrived on the Falklands, the Argentine military authorities were distributing leaflets to the soldiers warning them they were on their way and describing, with some accuracy, their uniforms, equipment and way of operating. Later, fear of the SAS turned to paranoia. One day in Port Stanley the military police rounded up a group of civilians and searched them for weapons, thinking that the SAS might have disguised themselves as kelpers and infiltrated the town. A story went round the garrison that a forward patrol had been found with their throats cut, evidence it was said of the SAS. In fact they kept their uniforms on during the war for fear of sparking reprisals against civilians. The patrols who went ashore three weeks in advance of the landings avoided all contact with the Falklanders because it was thought they could not be trusted.

The SAS were the campaign's most enigmatic figures. Proximity to legends tends to diminish them, yet after ten weeks the soldiers and civilians who lived alongside the SAS still held them in awe and they maintained a violent chic that their Marine rivals, the Special Boat Squadron, never quite managed. Their style owed much to the character of their colonel. His background was a mixture of utter conventionality relieved by mildly exotic touches. His father was in the Indian Army, the fourth generation of the family to belong. He went to Cheltenham, then in 1960 to Saint Edmund's Hall, Oxford, where he read Politics, Philosophy and Economics. In his spare time he amused himself by learning to fly, collecting English water-colours and mounting a large art exhibition.

He spent a year teaching in France and then bowed to the inevit-able and joined the Coldstream Guards. After stints in Aden and Northern Ireland he joined the SAS and spent two years in the Middle and Far East seeing action in Oman. He returned to the SAS in 1979 and commanded it for a period when, thanks to the Iranian embassy siege, it ceased to be merely a military unit and became a metaphor for efficient violence, in which Britain, rather short of heroes, took an inordinate pride.

To the journalists with the task force he made a change from the average officer. The bookshelf in his cabin carried *Brideshead Revisited, The Golden Bough* and *Earthly Powers*, though it was unkindly suggested these had never been opened. Unlike many of the other task force brass who were always ready with a maxim from Wellington or von Clausewitz he claimed to have no military heroes. Some of the SAS men we encountered had been on the islands for more than a month by then, leading an extraordinarily harsh and solitary existence. They seemed remarkably normal for all that. One of them greeted us later on: 'I know you, don't I? I think you know my sister.' Under the stubble and uniform, a rather diffident kindly man remembered from London drinks parties came back to mind.

The SAS were aggrieved at their macho image. 'The SAS man is not a gorilla, locked up in a cage who one lets out when one wants a bit of violence created,' said an officer. 'They are realists; quiet people who have a lot of confidence in themselves because they have been through a selection system that weeds out the braggarts and the romantics.' The average age of the men was twenty-eight – old for the Army. Many of them came from poor or broken homes. Rank differences in the SAS were much less marked than in other units, partly because the men have a large say in choosing their officers and because no distinguishing insignia were worn. This led to some disquiet among the more protocol-conscious naval officers back on the ships. Frequently they suspected that the piratical-looking men drinking in the wardrooms of their ships were not officers, but in the circumstances they were wisely reluctant to press the matter. Unlike the rest of the Army the SAS was allowed to choose its own weapons and equipment. At the start of the war it carried, like the SBS, American-made Armalites which weigh considerably less than the ten-pound standard self-loading rifle. Later in the campaign some SAS men swopped back to the SLRs following an incident where an Argentine soldier was still firing back after being hit seven times by rounds from an Armalite.

The SAS were obsessional about kit. One of them spent the morning HMS *Antelope* went down touring San Carlos Water in a rubber dinghy sifting through the flotsam. He picked up a sodden sleeping bag, dried it out and slept in it from then on. 'Great bit of kit,' he said. On one occasion two SAS men were seen bartering over a polo-neck pullover which eventually changed hands for two hand-grenades, which were carefully placed at the bottom of a bergen. Their most impressive piece of kit was a portable communications satellite which went up Mount Kent with them. One morning I saw an SAS man crouched below a rocky bluff talking to his friends in Hereford 8,000 miles away. Some of the SAS affected to be rather unimpressed by the war, treating it as an unchallenging routine operation. When they got to Port Stanley they quickly got bored waiting for transport home and were planning to march right across East Falkland from San Carlos, merely for something to do. The exercise was abandoned, reluctantly, because of the danger from mines.

In contrast, the SBS kept a lower profile. Their first operation came during the re-taking of South Georgia when fourteen of them in frogmen's suits swam ashore from a nuclear-powered submarine close to Grytviken. Like the SAS they went ashore on the Falklands weeks before the invasion, to map out the positions of Argentinian troops and check landing sites. They were recruited from the Marines – only one of every twenty-five is chosen – and reflected their obsession with physical fitness. One officer, a small fair-haired man called Simon who possessed a deceptively cherubic face, was said during training to make soldiers run for miles before doing press-ups in a river. 'I know they're amphibious troops but that's going over the top,' one naval officer commented. One of the SBS booties was also training to attempt the world record of 9,105 consecutive press-ups.

The 3,000 men from 5 Infantry Brigade finally moved into San Carlos Water on a misty morning on 2 June on board *Canberra* and *Norland*. The 1st Battalion Welsh Guards, the 2nd Battalion Scots Guards and 1/7 Gurkhas Rifles had left Britain on 12 May on the *Queen Elizabeth II* and cross-decked at South Georgia, 800 miles away, because of the air threat to the ocean liner. This had delayed their arrival on the Falklands by eight days. They left Southampton to an emotional send-off. 'I was with two other senior officers, all facing in different directions, and we all swore the wind was in our eyes,' a Welsh Guards major said. 5 Brigade, however, was unsure of its role in the South Atlantic; uncertain if it was going to fight or be a garrison. War had broken out but there was still a chance of a diplomatic settlement.

The brigade was assigned for a role outside NATO countries but only the Gurkhas were formally attached to it. Lt.-Col Johnny Rickett of the Welsh Guards had volunteered his battalion after they had finished their six-week Spearhead tour of duty, when they had to be ready to move in less than twenty-four hours to a trouble spot. The Scots had been asked on 5 April, the day the Navy sailed out of Portsmouth, to be ready in case they were needed. The two battalions normally part of 5 Brigade, 2 and 3 Para, had already left with 3 Commando Brigade. As the necessity of reinforcements for the heavily outnumbered 3 Brigade became more apparent, 5 Brigade was sent off for ten days' training in Wales at the end of April.

As on *Canberra* the two-week voyage to South Georgia was taken up with planning and weapon training. By all accounts the Gurkhas had a nervous time, obsessively practising for lifeboat drill wearing blindfolds so they could escape from their cabins in darkness. The ship was joined at Ascension by Maj.-Gen. Jeremy Moore, who until then had operated from Northwood. With him came his staff of military advisers, intelligence officers and interpreters. One of them, still wearing his tweed jacket, was heard ruminating over what rank he should assume. 'I can't be a captain because that doesn't carry enough weight,' he said. 'On the other hand a colonel seems a bit strong. I think I'll be a major.'

The Guards were sensitive to any suggestion they were ceremonial troops and were proud of their long fighting tradition. But there was a difference between them and the Marines and Paras. Unlike the Marines they were not so obsessed with physical fitness and they had none of the undercurrent of violence associated with the Paras. On shore they never looked quite as neat as the Marines, or indeed, quite as tough. When they arrived at San Carlos the air raids had ceased for a time and they did not dig in with the same vigour. Having seen both the Marines and 5 Brigade coming ashore the difference was quite marked. But this did not detract from their fighting qualities. They were just as eager to have a go at the

Argentinians and in one air raid on Bluff Cove the Scots Guards fired 18,600 rounds, an average of thirty a man, claiming to have downed two Skyhawks. On Tumbledown the Guards used steel, after they had run out of ammunition. One major, said to be a peace-loving man fond of Beethoven, bayonetted two Argentinians. The officers had a deceptively languid air, particularly the aristocrats among them, but they knew their jobs.

Once 5 Brigade had come ashore the plan was for them to join up with 2 Para at Goose Green and Darwin and move round from the south in a pincer movement with the Commandos in the north. It would have been a time-consuming slog across harsh terrain but for a spectacular advance to Bluff Cove and a decision to take the men round by ship. Brigadier Tony Wilson was in an ebullient mood at San Carlos on 3 June. Standing in his green Wellington boots in a blustery wind and surrounded by piles of ammunition, anti-tank guns and filing cabinets, he enthused: 'I'm moving people forward as fast as I can with stocks of ammunition to launch what I suppose could be called the final offensive. I've grabbed fifty-five kilometres in this great jump forward and I want to consolidate it.'

It was a move which demonstrated Wilson's flair and military opportunism. He won his Military Cross in Northern Ireland and claimed to have seen action in every rank he had held in the Army. He had heard there was a telephone link between Swan Inlet and Bluff Cove and had sent two armed helicopters from Darwin containing Paras to telephone ahead and discover if there were any Argentinian troops at the settlement. It was here the myth of the 50p piece telephone call originated. Islanders told the Paras there were no Argentinians so the decision was taken to move everyone forward as fast as possible to catch up with 3 Brigade.

'It sounded a golden opportunity,' Wilson said. 'I thought it was a now or never chance because they could come back during the night. Unless I took a chance I might end up fighting for Fitzroy or Bluff Cove and only a fool would fight for a place he could have taken for nothing.' It also saved him marching men across open country in view of Argentinian observation posts which could call in artillery and air strikes.

2 Para were once again the vanguard, moving into the tiny hamlet of Bluff Cove short of rations and living off mutton killed for them

by a local farmer, a former barrister from Britain. The troops came in by a Chinook, not knowing if they would be hit by planes, artillery or a counter-attack. In the event nothing happened and the Argentinians did not seem to know they were there. The Gurkhas meanwhile had moved up to Goose Green to guard prisoners. This caused near panic among the Argentinians who had heard terrifying stories of small, slant-eyed men who slit their victims' throats with kukris.

It was at Darwin, just a couple of miles from Goose Green, that a peripatetic pig had developed the alarming habit of scratching its bottom against a 1,000 pound unexploded bomb two hundred yards from the settlement. The same pig ventured into a barn where Guardsmen were sleeping. 'That fucking pig came in here and parked its arse on my head last night,' I heard one of the men complain. 'Never mind lad,' his sergeant replied. 'It'll soon get used to the smell.'

The Brigade HQ was set up in an empty house. Paper signs written in felt-tipped pens had been hastily stuck on doors with messages such as 'Out of Bounds' or 'AQ Ops'. Officers stomped around in their heavy boots looking for light bulbs or removing maps and secret signals from a safe sitting on the kitchen table. General Moore was having a briefing with Wilson and said he had gone up to Mount Kent to look at Port Stanley for the first time but 'the blasted cloud prevented me from seeing it'. He praised 5 Brigade's leap forward and said: 'You either get ashore and move steadily or you go like hell across the island. 5 Brigade went like the clappers and now we have to roll up our logistics.' The Brigadier was staying at the house of the general manager of the Falkland Islands Company and would sit up late in the evening writing out orders, occasionally coming into the kitchen saying 'hello pussycats' to the moggies. Two kelpers arrived from Lafonia, where the Gurkhas were scouring the land for renegade Argentine groups, and said they had helped an Argentine pilot who had bailed out after being shot down. The man had parachuted into Falkland Sound and swum ashore where he spent the first night wrapped in seaweed, the second lying in the 'diddle-dee' or Falkland heather and the third in a farmhouse. The kelpers had found him suffering from neck and groin strain from when he had ejected and had called in the Argentinians to take him to hospital. 'He seemed a nice chap,' they said, as if they were surprised he didn't have two horns and a tail.

The original plan for the southern advance was for the Guardsmen to march or be helicoptered to Darwin, and then move overland towards Bluff Cove and Stanley. The Welsh Guards had tried marching over Sussex Mountain but the weather clamped down and they were forced to return to San Carlos. Given the shortage of helicopters, Wilson then decided to take the risk of bringing the men round by ship. To have marched them could have lost the whole momentum of the campaign. The two battalions were due to come ashore in landing craft from *Intrepid* at Bluff Cove on 6 June but only the Scots moved in, spending seven hours in open LCUs in rough seas and getting thoroughly wet. The Navy, alarmed by the threat of land-based Exocet missiles, offloaded them near Lively Island, about thirty miles south of Bluff Cove. The drenching they received gave many of them exposure and trench foot. The Welsh Guards came round on 7 June for a similar offshore landing but when they lined up on *Fearless* for disembarking they found there were two LCUs instead of the arranged four. The other two were said to be off Bluff Cove. As a result only the headquarters' staff, 2 Company, a machine gun and anti-tank platoon got ashore and took up position slightly forward of the Scots Guards. The rest of the battalion had to return to San Carlos.

This was the start of a series of errors and ill fortune which was to lead to the disaster on board *Sir Galahad* when fifty men died in the worst single loss of British life in the war. The remainder of the battalion back in San Carlos – about 300 men – was embarked on *Sir Galahad*, a Royal Fleet Auxiliary ship of 5,700 tons with a largely Chinese crew. The vessel was due to bring the men round Lafonia overnight and land them soon after dawn on 8 June. Welsh Guardsmen, however, were late boarding the ship and she only sailed at midnight. As a result *Sir Galahad* arrived at Fitzroy at dawn when the two LCUs were being used to take ammunition off the supply vessel *Sir Tristram*. The absence of air attacks for the past ten days seemed to remove any sense of urgency and the Guardsmen had to sit on the ship for several hours in broad daylight playing cards and watching films on television, waiting for transport ashore. The Navy claimed the delay was caused by the Welsh Guards refusing to go in an LCU carrying ammunition or on to beaches which had not been checked for mines.

Wilson had arranged for air cover for a set period after dawn, but no one told the fleet the Guardsmen had been delayed and the Harriers returned to the aircraft carriers at the arranged time, leaving no protection. As a second line of defence four Rapier units had been set up round the settlement. But these notoriously sensitive weapons had not been given the twenty-four hours they needed to stabilize and when the attack came they either misfired or missed. Perhaps the worst breakdown in communication came with the failure to alert the ships and units that an air raid was imminent. For some twenty minutes before they bombed *Sir Galahad* and *Sir Tristram* it had been known that enemy planes were approaching the Falklands. They were located on radar but disappeared for five minutes over Lafonia. In such cases the standard procedure was to alert all units, but the message did not get through. Even if adequate warning had been given, there was no direct radio communication between 5 Brigade's HQ in Fitzroy and the ships half a mile out in the bay. Lt.-Col Mike Scott of the Scots Guards said they received a red air alert only moments before five Skyhawks swept by hugging the valley after they had hit the ships. A company of Welsh Guards further forward opened fire.

The bombs from the Skyhawks hit *Sir Galahad* through the engine room at the stern and the accommodation section. One failed to explode and blasted through the other side, just missing a long-awaited LCU which was now moored alongside ready to take off troops. But those that did explode wreaked havoc. Men were trapped below decks and received terrible burns. Many rushed across the deck pulling on bright orange survival suits and life jackets. Some jumped into the freezing sea to escape the flames, and even swum underwater to avoid burning oil. Inflatable rubber life-rafts were hurled over the side but some immediately burst into flames as they were hit by debris from the explosion. Others were blown by the wind into the burning oil. Ropes were thrown over board and men clambered down into the lifeboats. By now black, acrid smoke was billowing from the stern and huge flames leapt from the ship, setting off ammunition which exploded with sharp cracks. Sea King and Wessex helicopters immediately launched a gallant rescue operation, flying into the thick of the impenetrable smoke to rescue men. Winchmen were lowered into the sea to grab the survivors and haul them on board. At times helicopters were obscured by the smoke, emerging moments later with shocked and burned Guardsmen and sailors. *Sir Tristram* launched lifeboats which began taking some of the rubber life rafts in tow. Others started drifting towards the blazing ship. Helicopter pilots at the bow saw what was happening and brought their machines round to the stern where they used the down-draught of the rotor blades to blow the rafts to safety.

The narrow inlet of Port Pleasant was swamped with lifeboats, orange inflatable life rafts and landing craft. Hundreds of survivors staggered ashore. Many were badly burned and a shuttle of helicopters started ferrying them to Ajax Beach hospital, *Uganda* and several other vessels at San Carlos. 'I've never seen burns like that,' one doctor said. 'We just don't have the equipment to deal with them.' One dazed group of Welsh Guards, their hair singed from the fires, built a peat shelter when a red air alert was given an hour after the first raid. They moved slowly, like sleepwalkers, and were subdued as some attempted to crack jokes when their names were checked. Children from the settlement, oblivious to the air threat, handed them jugs of hot, sweet tea. One man quietly left our pathetically inadequate shelter and was sick behind a fence.

Overhead the Harriers returned to fly combat air patrol, leaving white condensation trails as they circled high above. A Guardsman started singing the British Airway advertising jingle: 'We'll take more care of you . . . Fly the flag.'

Andrew Pillinger, a young radio officer from *Galahad*, said he had been on the flight deck when the planes struck: 'The first thing I heard was jets coming over and then the bombs . . . two hit us, maybe three. I went back to my cabin but the smoke was so thick I had to feel my way down the corridor. People were screaming trapped in their rooms. They were in agony. There was mangled wreckage in the corridor.' The ship's purser, John Hood, said: 'I felt two thuds as if someone was slamming watertight doors. The lights went out and there were screams and thick black smoke.'

But that was not the end of it. A huge pall of black smoke as if from a funeral pyre hung over the bay as another Skyhawk swept in for attack. It was met with a hail of small-arms fire and missiles. Tracer bullets curled towards it yet it passed through the curtain of lead just a hundred yards from us. Instead of bombing or cannoning targets it peeled away, pursued by missiles. That Tuesday marked a full Argentinian assault. An LCU bringing 5 Brigade HQ's equipment was strafed, killing several men, and HMS *Plymouth* was bombed by Mirages in San Carlos. Soon *Sir Tristram* began to smoke, hit by bombs. She too was abandoned and burned into the night.

The full extent of the tragedy on *Sir Galahad* was not known for some time. Two days later the Welsh Guards were told they had lost only nine men and then the figure leapt to forty killed and seventy-nine injured. Twenty-two of the dead came from the mortar platoon, the same platoon that was to be struck by disaster when Sidewinder missiles accidentally went off at Stanley airfield after the surrender, injuring several Guardsmen. It was a tremendous blow to the battalion. 'We all knew one another very well,' Major Jo Griffiths-Eyton, the second-in-command, said later. 'We're like a large family and it hit hard. But everyone said "Well come on boyos. Let's go and pay them back." The battalion picked itself up remarkably well and it began looking forward.'

After Stanley had fallen, a memorial service was held at Bluff Cove and *Sir Galahad*, still burning two weeks after the attack, was towed out to sea and sunk as a war grave. It was a cold, cheerless evening, with the Welsh Guards formed up on three sides of a square. At the end a bugler played the Last Post and the choir sang the Welsh National Anthem, 'Land of my Fathers'. All that now marks the site at Fitzroy is a lone wooden cross bearing the crest of the Welsh Guards.

In retrospect, bringing troops round in *Sir Galahad* and off-loading them in daylight seems a risky operation. The ships, which were visible for miles, could have been seen from Argentine observation posts on high ground towards Port Stanley, and these could have directed the attacking planes. But at that time the lull in air attacks fostered a dangerous over-confidence. The Brigade HQ at Fitzroy, for instance, had been placed in the largest building in the settlement with electric light shining through the skylights all night. Wilson, clearly shaken by the raids, called a meeting of senior officers at midnight and the brigade started digging in immediately. By morning the HQ was almost invisible behind a hedge just outside the settlement.

Wilson was eager to bring his men up as fast as possible so as not to delay the assault on Stanley, especially as troops were beginning to suffer from the weather. He commandeered a small coaster called *Monsunen* to transport men and equipment from Goose Green to Fitzroy. It was rather a dramatic and swashbuckling gesture and it became dubbed 'Wilson's private navy'. Once the propeller had been freed from rope, this 230-ton little coaster, with a penguin painted on its funnel, set off with some of 2 Para on board. It was a brilliantly sunny afternoon, 'ideal for an air attack', as someone said. Just before she sailed a Gurkha officer came on board to say there was a threat of land-based radar-guided Exocet missiles on our route. Fox Point and Lively Island at the mouth of the Choiseul Sound were likely sites and the Gurkhas were scouring the islands for them.

'Personally I think it's a bit risky,' the officer said. 'But if we find anything we'll buzz you with a helo and you can turn back.' *Monsunen* sailed past a wreck of a Chilean brigantine and a motor patrol boat which had been cannoned by Harriers. In the distance penguins sat on rocks and porpoises played at the bows as she chugged along at a few knots. She was such an easy target it would have taken a cross-eyed Argentinian to miss. The Paras sat calmly on deck, cooking rations with hexamine tablets, and only rarely scanning the shore with binoculars. But on this occasion the troops got through and were now preparing for the final onslaught on Stanley.

6

The Last Days

When the troops moved on to the mountains, 3 Brigade Headquarters shifted to Teal Inlet. General Moore stayed on *Fearless* to
co-ordinate the separate thrusts of the Marines and Commandos in
the north and the Guardsmen and Gurkhas in the south. Teal was a
bleak but beautiful spot. Like all the other settlements on the island
it owed its existence to sheep. It contained the nicest house on the
island, a large colonial-looking building with wood-panelling, good
pictures and carpets and a conservatory. It would not have looked
out of place in the Cotswolds. Inevitably it was the home of the
settlement manager. Once Brigade moved, it was soon joined by a
disparate collection of camp followers. The rear parties of the front
line units based themselves there. The journalists moved up, partly
because it seemed a good place to gather information, partly
because we were not particularly welcome on *Fearless*.

Accommodation was short, but a couple called the Thorsons
allowed us to sleep in a toolshed behind their house. After the
mountains this seemed almost decadent comfort. The Thorsons had
other guests, a middle-aged couple who arrived from Stanley a few
days after the Argentinians invaded and stayed on. The lady was
called Chick. Her father had come to the Falklands from Scotland
when he was eighteen years old and stayed on. She had three sisters

and a brother who all moved to England as soon as they grew up. Chick was married to Walter, a member of the islands' police force for eighteen years who now worked at the airfield. 'I'd quite like to go and live in England, but Walter won't have it,' she said. 'We've been back home two or three times but he's not hot on it. He likes the wide open spaces.' Every night the four of them sat in the living room talking to the soldiers and politely acceding to constant request from the journalists for water or the use of the lavatory. It was a square room with lino on the floors and nothing on the walls. The main feature was a large stove that was usually festooned with drying socks. The Thorsons, like most of the islanders we came across, seemed to feel no urge to fill up the yawning hours of loneliness and boredom that the nature of their existence imposed upon them. No one appeared to read or play a musical instrument. No one showed any inventiveness in the kitchen. The mutton that was eaten morning, noon and night always came served up in the same way: roast with two veg. No one even seemed to have the inclination to do small jobs around the place. At Teal Inlet there was a gate with a latch which had clearly been broken for years. No one had replaced it or mended it. Instead a wire coat hanger had been looped over the gate post as a substitute.

One day a Royal Fleet Auxiliary ship, the *Sir Geraint*, arrived in Teal anchorage. Later in the day little groups of Chinese men appeared in the settlement walking around in twos and threes talking to each other with great earnestness. They all wore identical blue raincoats and had steel helmets strapped firmly on to their heads. They were, it turned out, galley boys and laundry men from *Sir Geraint*, who after days of being bombed and strafed in San Carlos Water had decided they had taken enough and walked off the ship refusing to go back until the war was over. We came across a couple hiding in some bushes and asked them what they were doing: 'Air laid, warning led!' they whispered. Of all the people in the task force, the Chinese received the least consideration. When a soldier urged them to return to the ship and think about Britain, they replied, 'Fuck Blitain.' The RFA crews complained they were 'mushrooms – always kept in the dark, occasionally showered in shit'. No one told the Chinese anything. Some of them started the voyage believing they were sailing for Cyprus.

Two days after Goose Green, General Moore had said at Port San Carlos that he expected his forces to be in position for the final push into Stanley by 6 or 7 June. It was plain by now that the date was too optimistic. All the forward movement had stopped on the mountains and military activity was restricted to night patrols and artillery bombardments. The Argentinians around Stanley were astonishingly careless sometimes. One day an observer saw a food truck draw up by some Argentine trenches on the outskirts of Stanley: 'The NAAFI waggon bimbled up, they turned out of their trenches to be fed and we started shelling them,' he said. 'It was so impersonal. We were just sitting there hitting them.'

The weather was bad for much of the time, though it could change in minutes, and the helicopters were finding it difficult to move ration packs and ammunition up to the front line. Life became dull. Even the air raids were few and far between and when they did come the Argentine Air Force avoided Teal Inlet. Every night we listened on Sony seven-band radios to the BBC news. There is a point half way through the bulletin when the newsreader pauses and says: 'This news comes to you in the World Service of the BBC.' All the items that follow are the sweepings off the newsroom floor. By the first few days of June, thanks to the Israeli attack on Lebanon, the Falklands story had sunk below this vital meridian. We were down there among disappearing Angolan information ministers and minor maize crop failures in Zambia.

On 7 June, the Para and Commando COs were called to Teal for an orders group with the Brigadier and given their objectives for the next stage of the campaign. 3 Para were to take Longdon. 45 Commando were given the Two Sisters, a long ridge with peaks at either end that lay in front of Mount Kent, and 42 Commando were to attack Mount Harriet, a little to the south of it. The bad news was that no date had been set for the operation to begin. General Moore was now opposed to the idea of one brigade pressing ahead on its own. The attack was to be a divisional one. It would not begin until 5 Brigade was completely ready so that the attack would keep rolling until Stanley was taken. In retrospect it seems probable that the Marines and Paras could have finished the war by themselves, but at the time there was a feeling that even two brigades were not enough. Most of the Argentine defences were thought to be concentrated on Longdon and Wireless Ridge, which lay directly behind it. On the southern and central approaches, Harriet and Two Sisters were not expected to give much trouble. Mount Tumbledown however, which lay between Harriet and Stanley, was. Intelligence reports reaching the General seemed to suggest that the Argentinians were mesmerized by the threat from the south-west. A map found in Government House, after the fall of Stanley, showed three Argentine marine battalions lined up along the southern shore near the town, as if they were expecting an amphibious assault to accompany the land attack.

The belief persisted that the Argentinians had reinforced West Falkland, or were planning to do so by parachute drop. Right up until the surrender there was great concern about the possibility of the Argentinians moving the war there. There was certainly no feeling at the orders group that the rest of the war was going to be a pushover. Nothing was going to happen until everything was in position. From then on the helicopters flew continuous missions up the mountains laden with shells for the six 105 batteries sited around Mount Kent.

The divisional staff approached the forthcoming battle as if it was a staff college examination. One officer described the operation as 'a real Warminster job'. Remembering what had happened at Goose Green, General Moore was determined that all the direct firepower available should be in position and fully stocked with ammunition before the battle began. Some of the soldiers got irritated with this perfectionism. 'There comes a point where you have to decide you've got enough beans and bullets and say, "OK, let's go,"' said one CO. Every day the attack was put off meant another day on the mountains for the Marines and Paras. Nor were 5 Brigade any more comfortable. At the time the orders group was taking place the Scots Guards were digging in at Bluff Cove. The rain, whipped up by a fierce wind, swept horizontally across the bleak treeless moors cutting through waterproof clothing and soaking the insides of the dug-outs. Guardsman Sean O'Hara offered advice to the journalists. 'You don't want to get into your sleeping bag or that will get soaked,' he said, so we lay there while layer after layer of clothing succumbed to the damp and cold. 'Don't go to sleep or you may not wake up,' he added, before dropping off himself. This was not exaggeration. The night before one Guardsman who was sleeping in a trench could not be roused in the morning. He was unconscious with exposure and had to be revived with mouth-to-mouth resuscitation. The worst cases were pulled into the shelter of a sheep-shearing shed. It reeked of sheep-skins and carcases. Inside it looked like a scene from Dickens, with candles flickering and muffled figures gathering round a large open fire to warm their hands, wrapped in fingerless gloves. The Guardsmen lay packed together in sleeping bags with barely enough room for people to step between one body and another. One of the exposure cases had been placed in a transparent plastic bag and lay there in just his long white underwear getting trodden on by passers-by.

According to Brigadier Wilson, though, the conditions were not a good enough reason for bringing things forward. 'You don't attack simply because you are wet and miserable,' he said. 'That's one way of ensuring failure.' The destruction of *Galahad* seemed likely to delay things even further, but instead the pace of the campaign quickened. The evening after the disaster we were told the attack would begin in the next forty-eight hours. On Friday Brigade HQ moved up behind Mount Kent and that night the Marines and Paras attacked the first row of hilltop defences that lay between them and Stanley.

The Paras' attack on Longdon was the first to start. Mount Longdon is an unfortunate shape for an attacking force. It is long, thin and craggy. The Argentinians had been there for two months preparing their defences and reinforced it with their best troops: snipers and special forces from 601 company, Marines, and the whole of Seven Regiment. It was claimed later by some of the soldiers that American mercenaries were among the opposition. The story was based on the evidence of men who said they heard English being spoken while they were lying wounded close to the Argentine positions. There was one report that two men captured on top of the mountain admitted they were mercenaries. What is far more likely is that the American accents belonged to Anglo-Argentines who received their education or military training in the United States.

The original plan was to attack the mountain from its northern and southern flanks, but the danger from Argentine gun positions meant that this was a reckless course and the officer commanding B Company, Major Mike Argue, decided to fight straight up the western side. After some equivocation, the Brigadier decided the attack should be silent, reasoning that a preliminary artillery barrage would destroy the element of surprise and waste ammunition. In the end the Argentinians were warned they were about to be attacked when one of the Paras trod on a mine. Together with Goose Green, the battle for Mount Longdon was the hardest fought of the war, but this time its importance was military rather than psychological. The Argentinians fought hard and skilfully. Clambering through the rocks the Paras had to face accurate sniper fire directed through image-intensifying night-sights. As each position was taken it became the target for well-aimed mortar and shellfire. The Paras were greatly helped in their attack by a precise bombardment of the top of the mountain from the warships out at sea and the British artillery, which sometimes came dangerously close to the advancing British troops. In the end though, it was machine guns, grenades and bayonets that drove the defenders back. Major Argue's report of the B Company attack conveys the grimness of the fight. 'The force moved up the ridge to the north and began to retrace their steps . . . After only thirty metres fire was opened up at point-blank range. The muzzle flashes were clearly visible to company headquarters but not to the forward troops. In this initial burst Private Crow was killed and Lance-Corporal Carver wounded. Much of the fire passed over and along the line of march and we were very lucky to escape more injuries. The officer commanding ordered that a 66mm [rocket] should be fired from his location at the rear so as to indicate the enemy position. Captain McCraken did this with enthusiasm. Despite this, Lt. Cox was still unsure where the enemy were but ordered the section to his rear to throw grenades knowing this would place himself in great danger, so that he could extricate himself and his radio operator. This happened and with the use of his own grenade he also withdrew a little way so he could observe the position. No more fire was being brought to bear from this position and someone reported that groans could be heard. To finally make sure all was clear, both Lt. Cox and Private Connery fired 66mm at the position and then ran forward firing their rifles. At the end of this action three enemy dead were found immediately, and more after first light.'

The battle lasted ten hours and the Paras lost seventeen dead and forty wounded. How many Argentinians died is not known. In the next forty-eight hours six more men were killed by artillery and mortar fire as they waited on the mountain to move forward to Wireless Ridge. All the dead were privates and NCOs. The Argentinians fought bravely on Mount Longdon but their defence was poorly constructed. 'They gave us the whole of the front of the mountain on a plate,' said Hew Pike later. They had no forward observation posts and no direct fire trained on the ground where attackers were likely to form up. After Longdon there was discussion among the Paras and in other units as to whether the attack would have been so costly if the defenders had been shaken up by an artillery bombardment first. As it turned out it could scarcely have done any harm. The much-valued element of surprise only provided the Paras with an advantage for the first half hour of the battle at the best.

45 Commando had an easier time on Two Sisters. The feature was too long for the Argentinians to defend seriously without committing a couple of battalions to the task. None the less they still had to contend with heavy and accurate machine gun fire from the rocks on top before they took their objective. 42 Commando decided to approach Mount Harriet from the defenders' south-east flank. It was not an original tactic but one which surprised the Argentinians who had the bulk of their guns facing west in the direction of the beach-head. The Commandos had to fight their way up a steep hillside and through a field of fire commanded by heavy machine guns among the crags on the mountain top. Once they reached the summit they fired Milan anti-tank missiles into the Argentine bunkers and the defenders made off down the northern slopes into a rock-filled valley that led back to Stanley. As they scrambled over the moonlit boulders artillery observers called down shellfire on to them to increase their misery. Looking around the Argentine positions after the battle it seemed incredible that the Commandos could ever have taken it. They were bunkered well in among the rocks, protected on nearly every side by a sheer drop and ringed by

natural gun emplacements that could fire on a huge sweep of land on either side. The position gave a perfect view forward of all the routes available to the British. If eyesight failed there was a portable personnel radar dish that had not yet been taken out of its box. There were heavy machine guns and rockets everywhere. Some-one found an elegant-looking Mauser 1909 pattern sniper rifle. Although they had clearly been on the mountain for some time they had not bothered with very complicated shelters. Even so, they were well stocked with comforts. Every soldier had a foam rubber mattress infinitely superior to the thin rolls of plastic given to the British troops. The ration packs were also much better. They came with large tins of corned beef and *chile con carne*, powdered fruit juice and *pâté*. There were little cakes of soap and disposable razors, letters and envelopes for writing home and even a miniature bottle of whisky. Their boots were high and had thick cushion soles and looked far more comfortable than the stiff, heavy things worn by most of the British.

The Welsh Guards were to act as reinforcements for the attack on Mount Harriet, with 2 Para standing by for Two Sisters. For the Guards it was their first task of action since *Sir Galahad* was hit and the spirit of revenge was in the air, tinged by anxiety. They moved off from their battalion HQ at a quarry near Bluff Cove at dusk on Friday. A Sergeant Major stood at the front as men marched by two abreast saying 'Give 'em fucking 'ell, boyos.' A Gurkha officer wandered down the line: 'Good luck to the Welsh Guards,' he said. 'Leave something for the Gurkhas in Stanley.' The march up the partly-constructed road seemed like a war film cliché. The only sounds were the tramp of hundreds of boots. No one spoke. Men cradled their SLR rifles and the camouflage sacking strips on their helmets swayed from side to side like a Rastafarian hairstyle. There was a smell of burning peat in the air from the shell blasts and high on the ridge one could see in the half-light the small flickering fires as Gurkhas cooked curry.

Although the Guards, reinforced by two companies of 40 Com-mando, had to move only nine kilometres up to their position near Mount Harriet, the march took several hours as they picked their way through a minefield. Messages would occasionally be passed down the long file such as, 'Slow down, the machine gun platoon is getting left behind' to 'For Christ's sake stop. We've lost the machine gun platoon.' One gunner had to be helped back after he broke a leg on treacherous rocks.

The first sign of the attack on Mount Harriet was a stream of tracer bullets climbing into the sky as they ricocheted off boulders. Overhead, shells purred from naval ships and artillery fire behind us heaped high explosive on the jagged outcrop of rock. It was almost continually lit by the dead white light of flares, highlighting shadows. At the base of Harriet the Welsh Guards and two companies of 40 Commando watched on a numbingly cold night. The air became thick with the acrid smell of cordite as flames enveloped the hillside. Through all this an Argentine Browning .5 machine gun kept firing. Several anti-tank missiles curled lazily towards it, exploding among the rocks, but the machine gun post was only silenced by a Milan wire-guided missile fired by a Welsh Guardsman. Shortly before dawn we saw what looked like the headlights of a car moving deceptively slowly over land and then out to sea. Within moments we realized it was a land-based Exocet missile fired at HMS *Glamorgan*, a county class cruiser which had been shelling Harriet and Two Sisters. She fired a Sea Cat missile in defence, but there was a bright flash and her guns were silenced. Although *Glamorgan* took a direct hit, only thirteen men died, and unlike the *Sheffield*, she limped away.

The capture of Harriet took about five hours. By dawn we could see over 100 Argentine prisoners being marched through the mist to our rear lines. A dozen prisoners were gathered at the base of Harriet and told in sign language to walk, not run. The Argentinians misunderstood this and thought they were being made to run and would then be shot. When the battalion padre appeared wearing his cross the prisoners cowered behind rocks, believing they were about to receive the last rites.

During daylight on Saturday the Guards and Marines withdrew behind a ridge out of sight of the enemy and dug in for the day. There was some desultory shelling of Mount Harriet and our positions but not enough to prevent the troops trying to sleep. Lt.-Col Johnny Rickett snuggled down in his sleeping bag on the Falkland heather. 'We should have been in Horseguards in full ceremonial uniform but we're lying here celebrating the Queen's birthday,' he said. 'We've just tuned into the World Service and heard them marching down The Mall.'

A young Argentine prisoner called Antonio was brought to the Battalion HQ, his shoelaces removed. He had been based on Harriet ever since the invasion at the beginning of April and said the Argentinians had been withdrawing troops steadily towards Stanley. The next morning the Colonel had breakfast with an Argentine Major whom he described as 'a good old-fashioned soldier who thought Galtieri was mad and war against Britain was ridiculous'. The Major said he believed the Argentinians would surrender after two more days of fighting. Argentinian positions continued to be attacked by Harriers on 12 June. They lobbed cluster bombs guided by laser from a hillside and the noise carried to us with a dull crash. Troops cheered. 'No one within 100 metres of those things survives,' one of the medical orderlies said with satisfaction. On Sunday, 13 June, the day before the surrender, the Welsh Guards came under fairly heavy Argentine bombardment, with shells landing every minute. The array of batteries behind us quickly replied. One could hear the dull thud behind us, the whirr of the shell overhead and the distant rumble of the explosions. It sounded like huge drums being beaten in the distance.

Sunday was bright, almost warm. Up at Brigade Headquarters behind Mount Kent, soaking sleeping bags were stretched out over the rocks, steaming in the sunshine. 'Don't leave those there,' their owners were warned by an officer. 'The Argie air might spot them.'

General Moore had moved up to Brigade to supervise the final stages of the battle and had called the battalion commanders over for a final orders group that afternoon. The next stage of the plan envisaged 2 Para, supported by 3 Para, moving onto Wireless Ridge, while simultaneously in the south the Scots Guards would attack Mount Tumbledown and the Gurkhas Mount William. All that remained after that, before Port Stanley, was Sapper Hill, which was to be taken by the Welsh Guards. Even now, with less than twenty-four hours of the war to run, there was no feeling of optimism or even that victory was in sight. Most people were expecting a vicious street-fight in Stanley.

At about 3 p.m. one of the signallers stuck his head out of a tent and shouted 'Air Alert Red.' By this stage of the war no one took much notice of the warnings and carried on with what they were doing until the planes actually hove into view. Perhaps in order to set an example, General Moore emerged from the camouflage-swathed tents of HQ and stood in the sunshine in a horseshoe of stones, known as a sangar, chatting to 3 Brigade's deputy commander, Colonel Tom Seccombe, who now carried a walking stick and was beginning to resemble a character from his beloved Waugh.

After five minutes everyone was preparing to go inside again when four Skyhawks flicked over the brow of a ridge a kilometre away and flew straight at our cluster of tents and aerials. It is a curious feature of air attacks that someone always feels the need to shout 'There they are!' even when this is quite apparent to everybody. The jets roared towards our sangar. Bombs gently detached themselves and floated down on parachutes and the air filled with the crackle of cannon-fire. Everyone but General Moore flung themselves on the floor of the sangar, as an explosion made the air wobble. The planes flew on. We got up, looking sheepish and laughing with relief. The jets hadn't gone though. 'Here they come again!' shouted General Moore, alerting the gunners who had just been telling each other how close they had come to hitting the Skyhawks, which had now turned over Estancia House and were swooping down for the next run. 'I really think you should get down, sir' said one of the staff officers, tugging at the General who was still standing up directing fire. More bombs dropped. The engines were so loud it sounded as if the jets were only a few feet above our heads. This time they went away and stayed away.

The tent where the orders group was due to be held was shredded by shrapnel. Had the attack been a little later the Argentine pilots would have wiped out every battalion commander on the island. As it was the British were very lucky not to have lost Thompson and Moore. 'They nearly destroyed the whole operation,' said Thompson in an aggrieved tone, who had been standing waiting at the landing site for a helicopter when the attack started. The Argentinians certainly knew what target they were looking for. A map discovered in Government House in Stanley shows a little flag symbolizing the Brigade HQ, stuck precisely on the position where the jets struck.

The Welsh Guards were due to move forward that night to act as reinforcements for the Scots' attack on Tumbledown. If that went well they were to attack two companies of Argentine troops believed to be south of Mount William. We set off soon after dark to follow a route used by another company only hours earlier round the base of Harriet. Within an hour though we had run into a minefield. Two Marines from 40 Commando had their feet blown off by the almost undetectable anti-personnel mines, which were no bigger than a jamjar top and had been scattered randomly from helicopters. Two Scouts flew in pitch darkness with only a faint green torch light to guide them to collect the injured men. Shells fell both in front and behind us. The entire battalion of 600 men sat down to wait and the man behind me said: 'Don't move. There's a booby-trapped white phosphorus grenade in the heather behind you.' The only reasonable thing to do was to eat most of the contents of our ration packs. During the more terrifying moments of the war it was best to keep busy. Here it was impossible. One false move and the next thing you knew would be a medic sticking a morphine jab into your leg and a helicopter hovering overhead. This fear was converted into hunger. All down the line of patiently waiting men you could hear the rustle of Garibaldi biscuits and Rolos being opened. When the man in front of you suddenly got up and moved off into the darkness you had to grab everything and quickly catch up, obsessed with wandering off into the middle of the unmarked minefield. I began to lose things in the darkness; first a glove, then another. Men spoke only in hushed whispers, as if talking might give our position away. The effect of the mines was largely psychological. Every step you took you felt might be your last, almost tip-toeing in a futile attempt to skip over the bumps.

The experience was worse for a forward patrol of Guards. They were moving in a single file through the minefield when shells started falling in a row ahead of them, getting steadily closer. They couldn't scatter because of the mines. For some unknown reason the last shell smashed into the ground thirty metres short of the patrol leader and they continued their 'tab' clambering through the craters and thanking all the saints of Cymru.

It took seven hours to move a mile through the field, with sappers at the front feeling their way by hand for the mines and trip wires.

Their methods were not sophisticated. An assault engineer went forward on his hands and knees, prodding with his fingers or a small metal rod about six inches long. Trip wires were detected by a piece of wire wrapped round a finger and the sappers then edged along, their arm extended with the length of wire hanging to the ground. If it swung back they groped around for the trip wire. We would stop for about half an hour and then move on a few paces. Where mines had been located by the trail the engineers had placed white tape, and medical orderlies stood at both ends waiting to tend to the men who strayed out of line. Not everyone, however, shared our concern with stepping precisely in the boot marks of the man in front. One Guardsman wandered five yards from the file to relieve himself. It was an act of bravado and won him jeers from his mates. Although the battalion was delayed for several hours in the minefield we were not needed as reserves for the Scots Guards and our forward patrol had found the Argentine positions south of William abandoned. We reached a crease in the land where we could see the battle for Tumbledown and settled down to wait for dawn.

By this time the battlefield resembled a vast, melodramatic stage set. Every few minutes the Argentinian guns were firing 'paralume' parachute illumination shells that sank slowly to earth, throwing the mountains into relief and bathing everything in flat white light. The din of the British naval and artillery bombardment was punctuated every thirty seconds or so by the whistle of descending Argentinian shells. Half the time the whistle ended in a dull 'plop' as the shell sank into the soft peat and failed to explode. Just below Mount Harriet 42 Commando's medical team had set up their aid post in an abandoned 'chacon' lorry container by the side of the track and surgeon Lieutenant Ross Adley and Martin Ward were preparing for the first casualties of the evening. Around midnight four Scimitars and Scorpions rumbled past, laden with Scots Guards on their way to a diversionary attack designed to convince the Argentinians that the main thrust was coming from the south and not from the west. A little later the offensive began. The side of Mount William, a cone of peat and rock immediately in front of Mount Harriet, began to flicker with tracer fire and the crash of guns and mortars grew louder and louder.

In the dark, though, it was impossible to tell who was winning and who was losing. After a couple of hours we heard the tanks coming back. The story came out while the doctors patched up the wounded. The Guards attack had started well. The Argentinians hadn't spotted them until they were right on the enemy positions, but in the firefight that followed two Guardsmen had been killed and several wounded, before the Argentinians ran away. The survivors collected the casualties and headed back to the road but on the way they blundered into a minefield. There were ten casualties in all. One man had been carrying his wounded 'oppo' on his back when he stepped on to a mine and both his feet were shattered.

They sat in silence while the doctors stripped away the blood-sodden boots and cleaned the worst of the shrapnel from the wounds. Because of the fear of attracting the attention of an Argentinian artillery observer and bringing down shells, they had to operate by torchlight. The light caught one of the feet. It looked like a joint of butcher's meat. The men were not even front line troops but a collection of rear echelon storemen and clerks, rounded up for the night and put under an SAS major. One of them asked for a cigarette. 'You've got a heart of gold, mate,' he said. 'You should have been a social worker.' He was silent for a while, then he started getting angry. 'Two dead,' he said. 'Two fucking dead. All for some pimple on the arse-end of the world.' Within an hour and a half of the casualties arriving the first helicopters flew in to casevac the wounded back to Teal Inlet. We carried a sergeant who had trodden on a mine out to the Sea King. Up until then he had been silent but as he was loaded into the helicopter one of the soldiers grasped his wounded foot to push him aboard and he screamed.

While we were waiting for another helicopter to arrive Ross Adley said: 'We're a bit further forward than we'd like to be but it's making sense at the moment.' A paralume floated down. 'The guys would have to wait a lot longer for treatment if we weren't here. Seeing a doctor early tends to settle the blokes down a bit.' Earlier on we had encountered some Guardsmen walking back from the scene of the fighting. 'We've had enough,' one said. 'Our officer is a nutcase. First of all he took us through one minefield then he wanted us to dig into another one that was getting shelled. We told him to piss off.'

Meanwhile, six artillery batteries of thirty 105mm guns and two naval ships with 4.5 inch guns were pounding Tumbledown, Mount William and Mount Longdon. One company got on to the western end of the long, barren ridge of Tumbledown without firing a shot, although they later came under mortar fire. The second company, the 'left flank', then attacked the central section and came up against heavy fire. For four or five hours Argentine snipers, machine guns and small mortars slowed their advance as they dodged from rock to rock. Seven of the eight men killed in the attack died on this assault and twenty-one were wounded, half of the overall total. At times there was fierce hand-to-hand fighting. At least two officers bayonetted Argentinians. 'They didn't have time to change their magazines so they used steel,' Lt.-Col Mike Scott said. One young officer, only four months with the battalion, took his platoon to the summit after his sergeant was killed and the company sergeant major shot through the hand.

Much of the battle took place under the dead light of flares. First the Argentinians tried to locate where the attack was coming from and then the Guards fired them to identify the machine gun posts and call in artillery fire. Each shell sent up a flash of flame and then the forces moved in. There was the chatter of machine guns, the crump of mortar and then pauses, with just the shouts of combatants. Part of the problem was that this support gunfire was not accurate enough to take out the positions. But after a while there seemed to be only one machine gun that kept firing. Although shell after shell crashed down near it, the red tracer continued to spit out at the attackers. The fighting only died down just before dawn, with Argentine snipers still sending bullets whining through the rocks. And then the resistance ceased.

Of the ninety or so Argentinians who had defended Tumbledown, many from superb defensive positions and dug-outs, about forty were killed. The Guards took thirty prisoners, several of them injured. Others had fled during the fighting. From the top they could see Argentine troops heading back to Stanley and they called in artillery fire on them to stamp home the victory. At one stage when things were moving slowly, Scott thought they might have to withdraw and attack again the next night. 'The old nails were being bitten a bit,' he said. 'If we had been held on Tumbledown it might have encouraged them to keep on fighting.'

The Gurkhas had meanwhile come round to the north of Tumbledown during the attack to assault Mount William to the south, but by then most of the Argentinians had fled towards Sapper Hill and Stanley. The Gurkhas had taken a number of casualties from air burst bombs and mines in the advance and were disappointed they had not seen more action to avenge their comrades.

After the Argentine surrender the Guards' padre, Angus Smith, spoke to General Menendez, the Argentine military governor, when he was being held on the ship *St Edmund*. He said that the two decisive battles were Tumbledown and Longdon. 'When I realized Tumbledown had been taken I realized the game was up and I had to surrender if my men were not to be massacred,' he told the padre.

The morning of 14 June left the British in control of the key approaches to Stanley. Both sides rested, the British in the hills and the Argentinians around the capital. Weary troops prepared for the final assault on Sapper Hill and the town itself. It was a bitterly cold day, with a thin winter sun occasionally blotted out by racks of cloud and snow flurries. Then the guns, which had kept up their haunting bombardment, fell silent.

7

Surrender

When Colonel Mike Rose and his interpreter, Captain Rod Bell, flew into Port Stanley that afternoon with a white sheet draped under their helicopter to negotiate an Argentinian surrender, it was the culmination of several days of British pressure. As Rose walked at a brisk pace to the secretariat from the soccer pitch to meet General Mario Menendez he saw a group of islanders outside the hospital, distinguished by a giant red cross outside. 'Is Alison there?' he asked. 'Yes,' a shy-looking woman replied. 'Well done, Alison. You've done a good job,' he shouted. Dr Alison Bleaney, the island doctor who spoke every day to her patients in the 'camp' on a radio link, had acted as go-between for the ceasefire.

For four days British forces, especially the 'psy-ops' or psychological warfare group, had been talking to Argentinian officers through the medical network, trying to persuade them to surrender. There had been initial resistance but Bell, brought up in Costa Rica, prided himself on understanding the South American mentality. He said there were signs they wanted to capitulate. 'I think like they think and feel like they feel. I knew what form of surrender they would take,' he said. 'At about 1300 zulu (gmt) on 14 June I spoke to the Argentinian forces and agreed we should talk after a ceasefire. They had not surrendered but it was obvious they would. They were about to put up a white flag.'

Rose's negotiations with Menendez and other senior officers lasted about an hour and a half. During these talks they could refer back to General Moore on *Fearless* and to Downing Street. Menendez also contacted General Galtieri in Buenos Aires to clarify the terms of surrender and to try and arrange the withdrawal of their troops. 'Menendez was obviously a very sad man but he's intelligent and realized he had to give up the fight,' Bell said. The Argentinian military governor at first refused to surrender West Falkland, where 2,000 troops were based. The British turned down the terms, demanding unconditional surrender. Bell was translating for Rose and converting the blunt demands into a form more acceptable to the Argentinians, stressing their bravery and fierce resistance. But he emphasized they were surrounded and further fighting was pointless. The argument was not lost on Menendez, still reeling under the double loss of Longdon and Tumbledown.

After they came to agreement, Rose and Bell went away to draw up the final terms of surrender. General Moore was meanwhile preparing to make his triumphant helicopter flight to Stanley to sign the document. He left Fitzroy, the HQ of 5 Brigade, at 11.10 in a snowstorm and arrived in the capital just before midnight. The signing was delayed for two more hours while the Argentinians pressed for better terms. They wanted 'Islas Malvinas' after the Falkland Islands, the removal of the word 'unconditional' from the surrender and to keep their weapons. Moore refused these demands except to delete 'unconditional' and allow the officers to retain their pistols.

They then signed the document. 'It was a brief and simple ceremony in an upstairs room of the secretariat,' Bell said. 'They were very cordial, very civilized. Obviously there was great pleasure and happiness on one side and sorrow and realistic appreciation on the other. They expected to be treated as gentlemen and they were treated as such.' Both Moore and Menendez shook hands, saluted and called each other 'sir'. Menendez had to evacuate Government House for Moore and was soon taken to *Fearless* where he was held prisoner first in the padre's cabin then in a spacious commander's quarters.

Although the document was dated 23.59 gmt, 14 June, it was not in fact signed until about 2 a.m. on 15 June. Afterwards Moore sent the following message to London and task force commanders: 'In Port Stanley at 9 p.m. Falkland time, tonight, the 14 June, Major General Menendez surrendered to me all Argentine armed forces in East and West Falklands together with their impedimenta. Arrangements are in hand to assemble the men for return to Argentina, to gather their arms and equipment, and to mark and make safe all their ammunitions. The Falkland Islands are once more under the government desired by their inhabitants. God save the Queen.' He then set off to look at the town and meet some of the islanders, who had been sleeping in the West Store for protection. Toasts were drunk and Moore was hoisted on to kelpers' shoulders, still uncertain if the ordeal was over. All over the islands Argentinian troops were throwing down their arms. At first there was apprehension that regular units might fight on but they all surrendered. On West Falkland 40 Commando, most of whom had stayed at San Carlos to deter a counter-attack from the west, took the surrender of Port Howard and Fox Bay. Some Argentinians there were said to have taken bones from dogs and grain from chickens because they were so hungry. The SBS flew in by helicopter to Pebble Island, the scene of the SAS raid on 13 May, to capture 144 Argentine troops who threw down their weapons with every appearance of relief and docility.

The British reclaimed a fragile community, its small world turned upside down by the invasion and the ensuing war. Many of the retirement haven homes of the settlement were holed and broken by the shelling. One pink clapboard bungalow had a huge gash in its roof. A small Union Jack fluttered on the window ledge. Fires burned fiercely on the Monday and the streets were still full of armed Argentinians. There was a profound feeling of anti-climax. The faces of the Marines and Paras were dark with dirt and tiredness as they marched into the outskirts of town. The troops stopped at the first big building they came to, gratefully abandoned their packs and waited to be told what to do next while an officer went inside to check its suitability as a billet. No one was to be allowed into town because of the Argentinians. The troops went inside to make cups of tea but British shells had landed on the filtration plant cutting off the water and the electricity plant had also been hit. They settled down in darkening rooms and began to tot up who had died and who had been injured. It was not the triumphant entry into the capital they had been hoping for but by now everyone was too tired to mind. The people of Stanley reacted to the liberation with the same enigmatic reserve that everyone on the island had displayed throughout the war. Some of the troops were given hot drinks and home made cakes, but there was no champagne and no bouquets under the tank treads and none of the local girls were seen kissing the soldiers. Down in the centre of Port Stanley the British pickets eyed the Argentinians with curiosity rather than animosity. The soldiers were charitable about the Falklanders' self-absorption. They ascribed it to the months of occupation and the almost nightly naval bombardments. Unlike the inhabitants of Goose Green they had not been locked in but there was a sixteen hour overnight curfew and on the Friday before Stanley fell three women had been killed by the British bombardment, the only civilian casualties of the war. The guns shelled a part of town they thought was occupied only by the Argentinians.

The main priority for the British was to disarm the Argentinians and get them to the airfield where they could be guarded. Part of the problem was not knowing the size of the garrison. Argentine officers at first said they had about 15,000 men on the islands but this was grossly exaggerated and the true figure was closer to 9,000 with over 6,000 in Stanley. Long streams of men, dressed in drab olive green combat clothing, were soon marching out by Davis Street, past the dozen captured Panhard armoured cars and the shattered homes, curtains flapping out of broken windows. They queued up to hand over an astonishing assortment of weapons, forming huge piles of rifles and machine guns. One of the officers supervising it was Major Mike Norman, who was smiling. Locals ferreted among the hardware sorting out trophies and youths disappeared in the direction of town carrying huge machine guns in 'proffed' Mercedes jeeps. Officers from the fleet arrived to get their 'gizzits' or souvenirs. A Harrier pilot took off a rocket launcher.

Some of the Argentinian soldiers, their faces still blackened for battle, were sullen or defiant in defeat. One major said when we walked into Stanley: 'We shall be back, somehow and somewhere. With due respect for everybody in Great Britain we will be back because we know they are our islands.' But most simply looked pleased they were alive and the fighting was over. The difference between the officers and the conscripts was obvious. The officers were allowed to keep their Colt .45 pistols, as much for self-protection as honour. Soldiers spoke of the cold, the artillery and fear of Harrier bombing raids as their most abiding memories. They asked if *Hermes* and *Invincible* had been sunk and if it was true at least thirty Harriers had been shot down. When we told them both carriers were cruising up and down over the horizon and that only eight Harriers had been lost, some through accidents, they looked sceptical.

The airfield presented a desolate scene. The windswept runway and apron, only a few hundred yards from the ocean, was littered with wrecked planes. Nine Pucaras still armed with machine guns and rockets, had been destroyed in Harrier attacks, their noses dipping towards the ground in submission. One Italian-built Aeromacchi fighter sat on the runway, its cannon shells spilling on to the tarmac. Mingled among the warplanes were civilian Cessna and Islander light aircraft. Many were burnt-out wrecks. A huge bomb crater on one side of the runway had been crudely filled in with mud, the result of the first Vulcan attack. Another crater, at least twenty yards wide and fifteen deep, marked the approach to the tangled wreckage of a large hangar. The concrete terminal building was pockmarked by rocket fire and surrounding buildings had been gutted. Small groups of Argentinians stood around, seeking protection from the sharp wind. They erected makeshift shelters from bits of wood and corrugated iron and draped canvas on the wings of aircraft, awaiting their repatriation to the mainland. Although over a period of days they got cold and wet and were short of drinking water, the prisoners seemed relatively fit. A number suffered from dysentery but they all recovered quickly on board ship.

As soon as *Canberra*, now rust-stained and tired-looking, arrived in the outer harbour, the British started embarking the Argentine prisoners. They were marched the three miles from the airfield in long lines, some still carrying plastic bags of personal belongings and kit. Most of this was piled in the streets of Stanley as they were searched by Marines and Paras.

On a launch taking a group of prisoners to *Canberra* a sergeant asked how British troops thought the Argentinians had fought. We told him they thought some had fought bravely and others had surrendered quickly. He nodded, as if lost in thought and then said simply, 'It was the guns. They never stopped.' They boarded *Canberra* smiling and chattering, met by the curious and contemptuous stares of the seamen. There they were given soup, a roll and a cigarette with every meal. The liner reeked of peaty clothes and unwashed bodies.

However, *Canberra* was delayed from sailing by the Argentinians' refusal to end hostilities formally outside a fifty mile radius of the Falklands. But three days after the surrender Galtieri was toppled and the new regime hastened the prisoners' departure. At Puerto Madryn on the mainland the 3,000 soldiers were disembarked without ceremony. Only about 100 sailors watched and there was a brief ripple of applause as the first men clattered down the metal gangway on to Argentine soil. One man wept as he was embraced by his son. Most must have wondered what reception they faced at home. Back on the Falklands about 500 officers and NCOs were kept behind, bargaining counters to encourage the Argentine government to acknowledge the conflict was over. At first they were kept in houses in Stanley and then taken to San Carlos Bay. Menendez was one of those detained, moving from *Fearless* to the ferry *St Edmund*, where he told a British officer an uncertain fate awaited him at home. All were eventually sent back.

Stanley was littered with Argentine weapons. Troops discovered Sam 7 and land-based Exocet missiles on the road to the airfield. When they tried to pick up the Exocets they found they were still armed and pointing at Government House. If someone had pressed a couple of wrong buttons the island's military headquarters would have been obliterated. The standard of most of the weapons was probably better than British equipment, although it was not as well looked after. One engineer said he was particularly impressed by the Argentinians' communications and radar equipment. The sappers initially found three million rounds of ammunition and thousands of shells for the 155mm and 105mm guns. They discovered early-warning radar systems valued at £6m. each, Roland and Tiger Cat anti-aircraft missiles, land-based Exocet missiles for which the Argentinians were thought to have paid £500,000 apiece

140

on the black market, twelve armoured cars, about 150 Mercedes and Volkswagen lorries and jeeps and huge quantities of food and clothing. There were also a number of motor-cycles which the Blues and Royals acquired. Lt. Lord Robin Innes-Kerr toured the town on one as if he were surveying his country estate.

One shed was an arsenal, housing Sam 7 and Blowpipe missiles, TNT, fuses, mines, grenades and mortars. Many of the night vision aids, valued at £20,000 each, had been smashed. There were also fourteen helicopters found in Stanley, including two Augustas, which look like flying bedsteads, ten Huey Iroquis, one giant Chinook and a Puma. Some of the Pucaras at the airfield were salvagable and one of the few Argentine patrol boats that had not been shot up by Harriers sat at the quayside. All this equipment and ammunition finally quashed reports we had been hearing of a beleaguered garrison short of weapons and food. The Argentinians plainly had enough to fight and live on for several more months. Hercules, after all, had been flying to the islands with supplies until the day before the surrender. They were also evacuating men, among them the scores of Argentine journalists who had been covering the war from Stanley. One Uruguayan hack, who had stayed on in the capital after the British moved in, said they had grabbed their bags and left very fast. 'They were very afraid,' he said.

Most of the weapons, though, were incompatible with British equipment and were more likely to end up on the forecourts of regimental barracks as mementoes rather than on military manoeuvres. The food was quickly 'liberated' from its huge containers lying by the waterfront and it was common to find the corridors of islanders' houses packed with rather exotic Argentinian tinned dishes. It made a change from the mutton and two veg. 'We have had their food and smoked their cigarettes,' one engineer said. 'But the military equipment is an engineer's dream. It's rather like being a kid in a toyshop. We just want to play with it.'

The story of the occupation was beginning to emerge. One of the first people we met as we walked into town was Monsignor Daniel Spraggon, the buoyant Roman Catholic priest. He ushered us into his house behind his small church on the waterfront and gave us a cooked meal and allowed us to wash, the first time in two weeks. His house had twenty-seven bullet holes through the walls, fired by nervous young conscripts shooting at shadows. 'After the curfew they shot at anything that moved,' he said. 'They didn't know one end of the gun from another.' Displaying a thick book entitled *Moral and Pastoral Theology (Volume V)*, which had a bullet hole through the middle, he said: 'They got through that quicker than I did.'

Monsignor Spraggon was taken on the first day of the invasion to see the military authorities. 'I was told they had no intention of hurting our people but I told them I didn't care what their intentions were, they had done the damage already and they had left a mark that would never rub off. I told them that if they ever got these islands there would be no one left for them to rule. Who wants a dictatorship when you have the life of freedom and democracy? We have no real crime here, no poverty. There's no political violence. People don't get taken away. When they arrived they said there would be no change but they started changing things straight away. The radio station began broadcasting in Spanish and they brought in pesos and started driving on the wrong side of the road.'

The stories told by islanders revealed a frightened and jumpy garrison. The officers treated the men like an inferior species. While officers ate and drank from huge supplies of excellent rations, the conscripts scrabbled through dustbins looking for food to supplement their meagre diet. The islanders were full of dark tales about the 'goons'. One man said he had seen an Argentinian blown up by his own landmine close to his house. 'I ran outside to see this mass of blood. He got up, staggered and collapsed. His colleagues picked him up by his arms and legs and threw him like a dog into the back of an army truck. I presume he was dead.' The locals depicted the Argentinians as callous and indifferent to each other. One couple claimed they had seen a soldier machine gunned by his own men in the street, but at this stage one was disinclined to believe or disbelieve anything.

The bitterness and resentment caused by the occupation turned, belatedly, to aggression and in the days that followed the liberation was directed at the Argentinians queueing in the town waiting to board ships. They were accused of setting fire to some stores near the waterfront and wrecking the primary school.

They had certainly been responsible for smashing up the solid old post office, and the backstreets of the town were littered with Argentine excrement. But although fourteen local men were taken from their homes and sent off to West Falkland where they were put under house arrest, few inhabitants were ill-treated. It was an uncomfortable rather than brutal regime. A number were searched at gunpoint in the street. A sinister figure called Major Patricio Dowling, an Argentinian of Irish descent, made an appearance and bullied townsfolk. But no one ever claimed they were struck. Many of the Argentinians, including Menendez, were polite and behaved 'like gentlemen'. There were stories of looting but on closer examination this tended to be troops stealing buns from the deep-freeze or sleeping in beds with muddy boots. Some valuables and souvenirs were stolen and houses vandalized but the details of the outrages were vague. Most of the serious damage was done by the British shelling. One islander said without rancour that the British had caused more of a mess in Stanley than the Argentinians. Even the horse that grazed outside the secretariat throughout the occupation suddenly died in the road.

It was clear to everyone from the moment of liberation that the islands were going to change. The British troops were still arriving, men who had walked across the island with huge packs and weapons stomped into Stanley, their faces blackened. 'My most vivid memory of the campaign was seeing the trail of haggard, dirty and weary men padding into Stanley compared with the well-fed and sleek Argentinians,' said Thompson after the victory. They took over houses occupied by the Argentinians and the strain on the capital's crippled electricity and water supplies increased further. The town was suddenly full of troops in camouflage uniforms. They wandered down the streets, the Paras looking aggressive and the Marines smart; queued at the West Store to buy 'Nutty' and tinned foods, and crowded the few pubs and hotel bars. The locals did not seem to care for this. There were two queues for the store, one for troops and one for islanders. This meant islanders always got served before the soldiers. 3 Brigade imposed a curfew on their men to prevent them wandering around at night and they had to stay in their billets or tents. A notice appeared in the window of the Upland Goose Hotel stating that by magistrates' order no non-residents were to enter the bar. 'I get the feeling we're not welcome here,' one Para said.

The local sentiment against the Argentinians was beginning to spread to all outsiders. Ten days after the liberation a local woman was complaining that Paras had been in her house but had now moved out to board the *Norland*. 'You'll have to get the place fumigated,' a friend said. Des King, the proprietor of the Upland Goose, told Major Chris Keeble that he was fed up hearing stories about 2 Paras' exploits. He charged for his hotel, which had all the amenities of a Southend bed and breakfast, £20 a bed a night and put three to a room.

Slowly it was dawning on this remote little community, no bigger than a West Country village, that their former existence had disappeared forever. They could never again trust the Argentinians not to try another invasion and as a result would have a garrison there several times bigger than the civilian population. The attraction of life on the Falklands was its wildness and remoteness. But walking down its beautiful beaches and through its harsh landscape was now a thing of the past. The most disruptive legacy the Argentines had left was the mines. The scale of the problem was not immediately appreciated. It only became apparent as sappers had their feet blown off trying to clear them round Port Stanley. With the aid of Argentinian engineers, they estimated there were about 100 minefields between Stanley and Mount Kent. Thousands of mines lay scattered over the island, making it hazardous to walk away from cleared areas. They were the curse of the post-war Falklands.

The problem was that the Argentinians did not know where they had laid the small plastic anti-personnel mines. Some had been scattered from helicopters like seed. Others had been thrown over the top of trenches by soldiers, laying yet more mines randomly on top of other minefields. The Argentine maps supposedly showing where they lay merely confused the clearing up operations. Even finding steel mines, easily located with a metal detector, has cost the lives of 188 men in Britain since the Second World War. And these mines were carefully placed and marked on charts. The problem in the Falklands was on a scale never seen before. In Stanley a variety of measures was considered, none of which seemed very hopeful.

For every theory put forward there were obstacles. Setting fire to the peat, for example, would work efficiently but once peat fire had been started there was no easy way of putting it out. It could also 'go underground' and reappear elsewhere. Someone suggested driving sheep through suspected areas. The sappers were considering dragging chains from helicopters or fitting flails to tractors. But because of the tussocky land this would not guarantee clearance. 'I would feel I had failed if in a few years' time one little boy stepped on the last remaining mine on the Falklands,' said Major Rod MacDonald of the Royal Engineers. Sniffer dogs were even being considered. It seemed, however, that the answer could lie in modern technology. They could use aircraft fitted with infra-red devices to detect variations in the soil's heat where mines had been buried or a device that could detect plastic beneath earth. There was one form of conventional mine detector that was so sensitive it could pick up the tiny strip of metal inside the mine but it was too fragile for clearing large areas.

Another fear was that the minefields could jeopardize the Falklands' precarious economy. It would prevent shepherds rounding up their sheep in time for the annual fleecing, the basis of financial survival. It would also prevent islanders taking part in the traditional peat-cutting to secure a supply of free fuel for their fires and stoves. Unless a solution is found, the mines might well drive many of the settlers away from the Falklands.

Yet the aftermath of the war did not seem unrelievedly gloomy. For one thing the threat to the islands from the mainland had faded to nothing for the forseeable future. 'Argentina's claim is completely null and void now,' said Harry Milne, Stanley manager of the Falkland Islands Company. 'The British will never give this place up. The idea of independence for the Falklands is bloody ridiculous. How can we defend ourselves, 1,800 people in a country the size of Wales?'

Some saw the war as an unhoped for opportunity to reverse the economic decay and shrinking population that has afflicted the islands for decades. 'The future is pretty well tied up,' said Graham Bound, editor of the *Penguin News*, the Falklands' cyclostyled newspaper, 'before the invasion it seemed abysmal.'

'This place needs a change,' said one local. 'It's been going downhill for years and now it's like a village which has a motorway built in front of its door. The life we lead might be disturbed but it will mean a bigger harbour, new jetties, shops and restaurants and cinemas.' Liberation revived all the old dreams of supplanting the sheep as the islands' economic mainstay and replacing them with something more modern. Harvesting kelp to extract the valuable pharamaceutical chemicals; expanding the almost non-existent fishing industry perhaps or reviving exploration for oil, the lure that supposedly excited the Argentinians to pursue their claim to the islands so vigorously.

The less commercial Falklanders saw a future in the gentler sort of tourism, believing the islands could be promoted as an ideal holiday spot for ramblers and bird watchers. It did not matter that most of the schemes had been tried and discarded before. Within a fortnight of the liberation, plans were being made to bring the benefits of civilization to the islands. RAF engineers appeared at Port Stanley airfield to begin preparations for an extension of the airstrip to take fighter jets and airliners. Surveys were conducted to find sites for accommodation blocks to house the hundreds of maintenance personnel needed to serve them.

After a few days, a poster of Selina Scott, the newscaster, appeared on the wall of the Upland Goose Hotel, wishing the task force well. Most of the locals walking past had no idea who she was but there was no doubt they soon would. A small local television station, everyone predicted excitedly, would be one of the first benefits of peace. Many of them already had television sets. In an early attempt to win the islanders over the Argentinians had imported scores of televisions and given them away for a down payment of a few pounds. It was hoped that by tuning into the television on the mainland they would eventually be transformed into good Argentinians. Many homes in Port Stanley contained small gas fires, gifts from the invaders.

The lives that will most be affected by the presence of a permanent garrison will be those of farm labourers out in the 'camp'. Whether or not the islands ever get a cinema or a steakhouse, they will certainly get roads, something that up until now has not existed outside Port Stanley. To the middle-aged men and women of the settlements, who previously visited Stanley once or twice a year, that will make a difference, though perhaps not a very profound one. There is a hack phrase that is commonly employed to finish off newspaper stories about dramatic events. 'One thing is certain,' it goes, 'things will never be the same again.' It is tempting to say the same of the Falklands. But the place is so remote from modern life, so elemental, that it may take something more than a war to lift the feudal torpor that has lain on it for decades.

The islands feel as remote as they appear on the map. Their nearest neighbour is now avowedly hostile and home, as many still refer to Britain even though their families have lived on the Falklands for generations, is 8,000 miles to the north. To compound the remoteness some of them lead lives of unimaginable isolation. One Englishman who had emigrated there said when he first arrived he had taken a job as a shepherd in an uninhabited part of the islands. He was shown where the hut was on a map and set off in the autumn with enough supplies for the winter. He stayed there for six months and never spoke to a soul. His only company was the BBC World Service.

Most of the people on the islands lead an existence that disappeared in western Europe during the last century. The majority of them are employees of the Falkland Islands Company, the last of the nineteenth-century trading companies in the tradition of the East India and Hudson's Bay companies. The sheepshearers and slaughterers we came across seemed to an outsider to lead dismal, exploited lives. Many of them were single. They earned £40 or £50 a week and lived in bunkhouses, moving from settlement to settlement wherever the work was. Their entertainments were darts, cards and drink. Many of them rarely handled cash. Wages were paid directly into their accounts from which their bills for the bunkhouse were deducted. Once in a while they would draw some pocket money and go off to Stanley for a mammoth binge.

The focal points of each settlement were the managers' houses. In general they received a salary from the company that owned the farms as well as a percentage of the profits. Their residences were almost always the most imposing building of the settlement, sitting like a manor house among the flimsy dwellings. In communities where decoration was almost unknown, their houses were always carpeted and hung with decent pictures. The manager was also the person with the radio transmitter, through which the islands' medical service in Stanley kept in touch with the 800 people out in the 'camp'. So the labourers would have to go up to the big house for help. Few of the older ones seemed to resent the feudal structure of their lives, but the stirrings were visible among some of the younger Falklanders.

One of the effects of the war was to multiply enmities. Falklanders who had stayed in Stanley during the occupation spoke bitterly about those who had left the islands. Much resentment was directed at the British contract teachers at Stanley school who took up the Argentine offer to leave after the invasion. But those who stayed in the capital were objects of suspicion among those in the 'camp', who spoke darkly of collaboration.

To an outsider the Falklanders often seem curiously unmoved by the loss of life and property their crisis had produced. At times it was hard to believe they had any connection with the war. News of disasters, of planes shot down or ships sunk, was often met with mild headshaking and tut-tutting, as if they had just heard of a neighbour losing twenty sheep over the edge of a cliff. They would sit around their radio sets in remote houses bemused, as night after night the Falklands dominated world news.

Yet through all this there was an undercurrent of pleasure that they were being taken seriously and their once precarious future now seemed secure. To a seigneurial society the outcome could not be more satisfactory. The years of neglect were over and loyalty was to be repaid in full. At last the mother country was to fulfil its obligations as guardian and benefactor.

Epilogue:

Going Home

There was a scramble to leave Stanley once it was all over. The troops had had enough of the cold and the wet and wanted to claim the remnants of the English summer. The misery of the climate had been made worse by the knowledge that Britain had basked in a heat-wave while we had been away.

The problem was how to get back. Despite the fact the Argentinians had been landing C130s nightly during the war, the RAF were reluctant to start flying in until the runway was thoroughly safe. The outer harbour was crowded with a strange assortment of ships, many of them looking as if they should have been in Dover or Harwich. Once the last Argentinians had been seen off, 3 Brigade embarked, the Marines on *Canberra* and the Paras on *Norland*. 5 Brigade had to wait for the arrival of the garrison force, and their commanding officers immediately started lobbying the press to put their case for their own battalion to return first.

The journalists, however, were every bit as eager to leave. When a Hercules flight appeared unlikely, desperate ploys were dreamed up in the bar of the Upland Goose. These included chartering a seaplane from Chile, taking a hospital ship with the casualties to Montevideo and, most far-fetched of all, trying to leave via Argentina with the prisoners on *Canberra*. Others boarded RFA

Resource with the assurance she would reach Ascension within a week. The captain explained that his none-too-swift ammunition ship would have to do thirty-five knots to arrive in that time. Nevertheless a number embarked and once at sea were told there had been a change of plan and they were bound for South Georgia. They managed to get a helicopter back to Stanley.

Seats had meanwhile become available on the first Hercules which was expected to bring in Rex Hunt, the former governor returning as civilian administrator. It was decided the fairest means of allocating the limited number of places was by straw poll. When this was completed the list of the lucky journalists on the first flight disappeared and an extensive search had to be mounted before it was found, hidden behind the bar. Payments of several hundred pounds were immediately offered for seats on the inaugural journey, but none accepted. The fragile camaraderie which bound the hacks together during the conflict fell apart soon after we arrived in Stanley. No one had seen newspapers for weeks but when they arrived it quickly became apparent that some journalists had had a better war than others.

The pool system meant that every correspondent's report was available to anyone who wanted to use it. Max Hastings had been used everywhere, especially his account of being the first into Stanley. Some of his stories had even crowded out the reports of the newspaper's own man on the spot. Hastings also appeared to have produced three times as many words as anyone else, a tribute to his rapport with the military and his mastery of the labyrinthine communications. Some of the reporters took his triumph badly. Hastings nearly concluded the war being bayonetted by an irate correspondent who accused him of failing to file a dispatch he had entrusted to him.

For the hacks it had been a communications war: a constant struggle to get stories back to London. The Navy would have preferred a private encounter with Argentina with the occasional release in London to say South Georgia or the Falklands had been retaken. Reporting British losses was always fraught with difficulties and dispatches would arrive on newsdesks with gaps and words crossed out. On land we were preoccupied with survival: building 'bivvies', cooking 'scran' and taking cover during air raids. We became in effect historical reporters, reporting what had happened and avoiding speculation about what would. Some reports were so delayed, however, they became little more than footnotes to history. We had been warned, though. At the outset we were told there was a conflict of interests. Our job was to disseminate news, the ministry's was to suppress it. It was an axiom which proved all too accurate.

The Hercules must be the most spartan form of aerial transport ever devised. You sit, if you are lucky enough to get a seat, on a canvas bench, devoid of support, unable to talk to your neighbour because of the appalling din from the engines. There were some airline seats but these were occupied by the SAS. As we taxied to take off the crew explained that to balance the plane half a dozen of us would have to stand at the back otherwise the aircraft would not get off the ground. Because it was an 8,000 mile round trip to Ascension, the Hercules had been fitted with extra tanks in the cabin. Occasionally during the flight, one of the crew would peer into them with a torch to check the level of fuel. Some of the returning flights were enlivened with a mid-air refuel from a Victor tanker plane. As the top speed of the Hercules was the same as the stalling speed of the Victor, they dived through the air together for several thousand feet while the fuel was pumped through. The SAS immediately made themselves comfortable for the fourteen-hour journey. Some climbed into sleeping bags and snuggled down on the floor. One had brought along a hammock which he slung between the fuselage bulkheads and slept soundly for the entire journey. At Ascension we switched to an RAF VC10 and flew to England with the seats facing backwards. The countryside looked stunningly green after the raw and barren Falklands. The sight of shops and roads and terraced houses had a peculiar novelty and above all there was an absence of the green and brown camouflaged uniforms.

Only when we returned did we really appreciate the impact of the war on the country. To us it had seemed a largely private affair, insular and localized. Our horizons would be the next battlefield and the next day. We were largely unaware of what was happening on the political and diplomatic front. At times we had to remind ourselves that the outside world existed at all. Although we arrived

151

back two weeks after the fall of Stanley there was still a discernible mood of national pride and relief. People spoke of restaurants and cinemas emptying during the conflict as the nation became absorbed in the evening television broadcasts. No one had really expected a war and when it came it was met first with shock and then with resolution. The ecstatic welcome for *Canberra* was an example of the euphoria, an upsurge of nationalism which Britain normally buries beneath the surface. Every ship that arrived, however insignificant its role, was given a hero's welcome. It was not just families which went to greet them, but people who had travelled from all over the country. There was a sense of relief, too, that this small war had united the country rather than divided it further. Voices were raised in opposition but they were few and found little response. We were told when we got back that at one stage in June it seemed as if Britain were bound for a national resurgence not seen for years. The fall of Stanley, early success in the World Cup and the birth of Prince William seemed for a few days to herald a renaissance in national spirit. But it was a fleeting mood and by the end of the month people were relieved it was all over and went off on summer holidays to recover from the traumas of participating by proxy in the South Atlantic conflict.

The war, however, was not over for everyone. In Whitehall the first skirmishes were being fought in the campaign against defence cuts and the Falklands was a powerful new weapon in the military's armour. The Army had acquitted itself well using traditional tactics and the SAS had returned to their conventional role, similar to the one conceived for them in the desert war in North Africa. The Navy, however, had lost seven ships and was having to rethink its strategy. But the irony of the war for them was that their campaign against defence cuts may have been weakened by their victory in the Falklands. If they had been driven out of the South Atlantic the government would have had to take heed of their cries of 'wolf'. Despite their claims that if they had had early warning aircraft on a larger carrier none of those ships would have been lost, the government can argue that they did a job they are no longer designed to do.

On the way south we had received letters that at first were full of doubts about the wisdom of sending the fleet and the use of force. That gradually changed. People began to resolve in their own minds the ethics of the war and although debates continued about whether it should ever have been necessary, no one told us we were on a futile and ill-conceived mission. The arguments of avenging a wrong, expelling an invader and freeing an occupied people were too emotive. And the war had everything in its favour. It was neat and tidy. It had a simple motive and a simple response. It occurred with a startling rapidity. Most wars build up over a period of months or years; with this one we were at sea within three days and fighting within a month. Nor were we on a crusade against a traditional enemy. Few knew anything about Argentina and the hostility was directed at the regime rather than the people. All this would have changed if the winter war had dragged on with lengthening casualty lists and tales of exposure and trench foot. Speed was of the essence.

The battle for the Falklands was no major world conflict. The losses of 1,000 men were insignificant when compared with those in contemporary wars in the Middle East and in the conflicts of the past. Yet for three months in an English spring and summer the nation was in turn absorbed, alarmed, apprehensive and finally triumphant. It was a national drama and had all the cathartic effect of a Shakespearian tragedy, sating the resurgence of aggressive nationalism that seems to swell up with each generation.

When we got back people would ask us: 'But what was it *really* like?' The answer was that it was exhilarating and terrifying, full of periods of intense boredom punctuated by moments of acute fear. There was glamour alongside the horrors. Colonel H. died a hero's death and the Harrier pilots took on odds not seen since the Battle of Britain. The courage was of a high order and everyone involved discovered something new about themselves. It was a war of shadow and darkness, slashed by the dead light of phosphorus, of haunting bombardments and moments of blissful silence. And it was fought under the spectacular canopy of the southern hemisphere night. No war is to be wished for, but if they have to be fought, this was a better one than most.